The Lord of Victory

by LeRoy Lawson

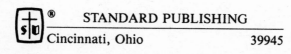

STANDARD PUBLISHING

Cincinnati, Ohio   39945

Unless otherwise noted, all Scripture quotations are from the *Holy Bible: New International Version,* ©1973, 1978, 1984 by the International Bible Society. Used by permission of Zondervan Bible Publishers and the International Bible Society.

Cover photo © COMSTOCK INC./Tom Grill.

Sharing the thoughts of his own heart, the author may express views not entirely consistent with those of the publisher.

Library of Congress Cataloging in Publication Data:

Lawson, E. LeRoy, 1938-
  The Lord of victory

  1. Christian life—1960-   I. Title.
BV4501.2.L3654   1988   248.4   87-26702
ISBN 0-87403-355-1

Contents

96953

Introduction

Knofel Staton has to bear some of the responsibility for this little book. Having read my *The Lord of . . .* books, he has urged me on several occasions to write one on *The Lord of Problems.* "Show how the Lord gives us victory over all of life's difficulties."

He began giving me this good advice several years ago. It has taken me all this time to summon enough courage to make the attempt. My delay has not been caused for lack of material on the subjects covered. My difficulty has been the opposite. There is too much to say. The first chapter is about fear. There's a book in itself, and a large one at that. The final chapter deals with victory in death. There's an even larger volume.

Think of the other life problems that the Lord gives us victory over: pride, prejudice, the god Mammon, rejection and loneliness, doubts, etc. So much to say, so little space to say it in. What's a writer to do?

This writer has chosen to limit himself to thirteen brief chapters, each one a meditation on one problem and its solution in Christ. If you feel dissatisfied when you finish, wishing that I had gone a little deeper and covered the material more thoroughly, don't think you are hurting my feelings. That's my opinion, too. My only defense is that my purpose in writing was not to present a thorough analysis of any one of the problems but instead to offer a brief reminder that there is no difficulty that besets us that we cannot triumph through in the strength of the Lord. Not the problem, but the Power, is the focus of each chapter.

Before venturing into print, I subjected my congregation to the thoughts you will read here. They are an honest bunch, my people, and they let me know what they think about what I think. I have listened and, when necessary, modified my preachments with their common sense. In a real sense, what follows is a collaboration. Sometimes you are hearing *me* speak; more often you hear *us.*

This cooperation is an often undervalued characteristic of the Christian life. We rightly sing, "There's victory in Jesus," perhaps erroneously implying that we have a kind of "me and Jesus only" faith, but a little reflection helps us realize that He often leads us to victory in and through the company of a great body of fellow believers. The longer I live in the church, the more I appreciate what being a part of the body of Christ has done for me. The Lord has often brought victory in my life through His people. In Christ, I am not alone; in His family, I have many brothers and sisters on whose love and wisdom and generosity I have come to depend. They have not let me down.

This reference to myself leads me to a necessary word of explanation about this author's intrusion in the following chapters. Many of the illustrations are almost embarrassingly personal. I have talked too much about myself on these pages. The nature of the subject seemed to force a more confessional style than I feel comfortable with. In attempting to persuade the reader that the Lord actually does meet us in our crises and provides the power for victory, it has seemed necessary for me to offer evidence from my own experience so that you will trust that I know what I am talking about. I have been there and have found Him there with me. The problem with testimonials like these, however, is that when we attempt to praise the Lord for what He has done in our lives, we talk more about ourselves than we ought. Please don't let my first-person accounts get in the way. The Lord is the subject; I present myself only as the object of His grace.

The sermon series from which these chapters grew was based on my favorite hymn, "It Is Well With My Soul." Since the congregation and the choir sang it several times during our study, it has become virtually impossible for me to read any of these chapters without hearing the words and music as I read. I hope you have the same experience, for what I have tried to assert through these pages is that no matter what difficulties life hurls at us, no matter how heavy the physical or financial or emotional burden we are struggling to carry, the person who is in Christ is always able and even eager to sing, "It *is* well, it is *well* with my soul."

He gives us the victory.

1

I Shall Not Fear

Luke 12:4-7; 1 John 4:18; Psalm 23

Neighbors in the Ukrainian village of Sarazhentsi found Pavel Navrotsky in his barn, a ghostlike, cowering figure in rags, his filthy beard straggling to his waist. Terror flashed from his barely seeing eyes as he peered into unaccustomed light. For forty-one of Navrotsky's seventy-four years, he had been hiding.

He had briefly been a Russian soldier in World War II. Very briefly. After just one day at the battlefront, he quickly threw in with the invading Germans. The Nazi occupiers allowed him to return home, where he lived peacefully until Soviet troops recaptured the territory in 1944. Afraid that he would be punished by his countrymen as a traitor for his earlier surrender to the Nazis, he disappeared into his barn, threatening to kill his wife Proskovya if she betrayed him.

She obeyed. Becoming a recluse herself to protect him, she barred all visitors from the place, locking the house whenever she left it to work on a local collective farm. Three times a day, she shoved food to him through a hole in the barn wall.

The system worked. Neighbors thought he was one of the thousands of soldiers missing in action in the war. Nobody suspected that he was near them all the time. Only once did he leave the barn, in the dark of night, dressed in women's clothing, but he became so frightened he ran back to his shelter and never ventured out again. He went undiscovered until his wife died and the neighbors came to go through her belongings.

When they found Navrotsky, he was terrified that the authorities would punish him. He had no need to be concerned. They realized that they could not have invented any torture that would have punished him as much as his fear already had.

Fear. What terrible things it does to us. A six-year study of American mental health completed in 1984 concluded that one in five Americans is mentally or emotionally disturbed, and that the

7

most common disturbance is anxiety disorder. No wonder when God speaks through His messengers, He has them begin with the calming words, "Do not be afraid." We need the reassurance.

Not all fear is negative, of course. The deer survives in the forest, the cat in the city, and the rabbit in the field through instinctive fears that protect them from harm. We similarly teach our children not to accept rides from strangers or play in the streets or eat food that has dropped on the floor. Jesus warns us to "be afraid of the One who can destroy both soul and body in hell" (Matthew 10:28). Some fears are good for us. But not most of them.

What Do You Fear?

A 1984 *Psychology Today* survey found out that what people are most afraid of is losing a loved one. This isn't surprising news. A well-known stress test lists this item as the most stressful experience a person can endure. The *PT* survey discovered that the next most threatening is serious illness, which is followed in turn by financial worries and fear of nuclear war. (By the way, the survey also turned up this fascinating tidbit: people are more afraid of spiders and snakes than of losing their jobs. One person wrote, "The Russians could place me in a room, release a couple of snakes and I would tell them anything."[1])

Afraid of the Loss of a Loved One

Who hasn't dreaded the ringing doorbell, the stranger standing there, somber in dress and demeanor, uttering those frightening words, "I'm sorry to inform you . . ."? What parent hasn't paced the floor at night, long after the son or daughter should have come home, fighting the unfounded conviction that there must have been an accident? Who hasn't grasped the hand of a dying loved one in a desperate struggle to hang on as life ebbs away?

Death scares us.

So does divorce. If you've been through one, you don't have to be told how much like death it is. "I don't love you anymore. I want out. This marriage is dead." The words sound too much like, "I'm sorry to inform you. . . ."

Afraid of Losing Health

If we manage to escape untimely accidental death, this is a loss we'll all experience eventually. What is worse than loss of health, however, is the fear of losing health. David Schwartz[2] addresses this

8

fear in one of his books. He had just finished conducting a motivational seminar when a young man of about thirty asked to speak to him privately. When they were alone, he explained to Schwartz that his ideas couldn't do him much good. He suffered from a bad heart, he said, and had to hold himself in check. He had seen four doctors, but they couldn't find his trouble.

Schwartz added his own prescription on the spot. He suggested that the man go to the best heart specialist he could find and accept his diagnosis as final. He needed to put a stop to his doctor-hopping. Then Schwartz pointed out that three out of every four hospital patients are being treated for illnesses that are caused by unhealthy emotions. Finally, he made his most important suggestion: "Resolve to live until you die."

Dr. Schwartz had to leave to catch a plane to his next appointment. After he belted himself in the seat, he heard a ticking sound. His seatmate, seeing the puzzlement on Schwartz's face, grinned. "Oh, it's not a bomb. It's just my heart." Twenty-one days before, he had received a plastic valve implant, he said, and the ticking sound would continue for a few more months until new tissue had overgrown the artificial valve. Schwartz asked him about his future, and the man spoke expansively of his plans to study law and eventually get into government work. He wasn't going to let his heart trouble get him down.

Two men with heart trouble. One, a cripple; the other, a person filled with anticipation because he had resolved to live before he died.

Can you stand my citing yet one more survey? This one concludes that only six percent of the American people do *not* have some health complaint. Forty percent of us suffer from chronic diseases and disabilities (these are the ones that just won't go away, no matter what we do), and most of the rest of us break down from time to time. Only one out of twenty seems to be filled with high energy and robust health. Wasn't it Winston Churchill who wisely observed, "Most of the world's work is done by people who don't feel very good"?

I asked the members of my congregation one Sunday morning to raise their hands if they had some form of ongoing complaint for which they were taking medicine or which they had to accommodate by curtailing some of their activities. I'm confident that more than forty percent responded. I told them they had convinced me I needed to move to a healthier climate!

In our church, at least, the question we must answer is not, "Do I have some illness that needs treatment?" Most of us do. Our real concern is this one: "Will I give in to my fears or will I rise above this illness to live a wholesome, satisfying life? Will I live before I die?"

Afraid of the Loss of Things

It's easy to put too much value in our possessions, isn't it? Frequently on television news, as victims of a storm or flood or fire or theft are interviewed, they will say, "I don't know how I can go on. I've lost everything." Yet that isn't true. They have lost their possessions, but they still have their bodies, their minds, their influence, their associations, their occupations, and, one would hope, their faith. If they have lost everything, then their tragedy is greater than they know, since they have made their "things" their all.

The Buddha is quoted as having said, "The less you have, the less you have to worry about." Jesus said it much more graphically, "Do not store up for yourselves treasures on earth, where moth and rust destroy, and where thieves break in and steal. But store up for yourselves treasures in heaven, where moth and rust do not destroy, and where thieves do not break in and steal. For where your treasure is, there your heart will be also" (Matthew 6:19-21).

When two thousand young men were asked, "What are your greatest concerns for the future?" they collectively said they were the fear of not having enough money, and fear of being locked in by the constant pursuit of money. The two worries go together, don't they? If you define success or security in monetary terms, then you'll seldom feel you have sufficient, so you'll drive yourself to get more.

Afraid of Being Found Out

Even a short few years ago, I wouldn't have mentioned this fear because I thought I was the only person who suffered such anxiety. Only recently have experts begun writing about "the imposter syndrome." They claim that seventy percent of all successful individuals are afraid of being found out. This is especially true of young achievers who quickly rise to prominence in their fields. They can't help feeling that if other people knew the truth about their weaknesses and inadequacies, they would lose their jobs and be publicly disgraced. They consider themselves imposters. Most of these fearful people are perfectionists who can never meet their own high standards, so they are convinced that they are failures, in spite of their apparent success.

Afraid of Almost Everything

I don't need to keep listing fears, do I? If you'd like a list, here's one from my dictionary:

acrophobia (fear of high places)
agoraphobia (of open spaces)
aichinophobia (of sharp objects)
androphobia (of men)
apeirophobia (of infinity)
astraphobia (of thunderstorms)
astrophobia (of stars)
autophobia (of self, of being alone)

That's enough. I'll quit with the a's. If I tried to name all of our fears, this would be too long a book.

If I did list them all, though, you'd probably find your special one here. Remember: the question is not whether you have fear, but whether your fear has you. That's really what this introduction is about.

What Will You Do About Your Fears?

I am going to offer you four resolutions for coping with your fears. If you will adopt them as your own, you can experience victory in the Lord. Each of them is drawn from Scripture, just as each of the following chapters is. Each is also derived from my personal experience. I'm passing on to you principles that I have tried to live by. When I've held on to them, they have not failed me. (I wish I could say that I have never failed them, but that wouldn't be quite true.)

Here is the first:

I Will Fear God and No Other

Jesus is sending His disciples out on their trial mission. Encouraging them to be bold, He charges them to fear only God; then they won't have any reason to be afraid of anything or anyone else.

I tell you, my friends, do not be afraid of those who kill the body and after that can do no more. But I will show you whom you should fear:

Fear him who, after the killing of the body, has power to throw you into hell. Yes, I tell you, fear him. Are not five sparrows sold for two pennies? Yet not one of them is forgotten by God. Indeed, the very hairs of your head are all numbered. Don't be afraid; you are worth more than many sparrows (Luke 12:4-7).

Jesus meets their primary anxiety head-on: don't be afraid of dying. There is something worse than death. Be afraid of that. There is Someone greater than death. Be afraid of Him. Christians are not ashamed to admit that they fear the Lord. Here's an early description of us: "Then the church throughout Judea, Galilee and Samaria enjoyed a time of peace. It was strengthened; and encouraged by the Holy Spirit, it grew in numbers, living in the fear of the Lord" (Acts 9:31). It was their attitude toward God that enabled Peter and the rest of the apostles to resist civil authorities ("We must obey God rather than men!" Acts 5:29). They had no doubt that the One who was in them was "greater than the one who [was] in the world" (1 John 4:4), so they feared Him only.

The worst that can happen to a person, it is commonly believed, is to be killed. This is not the Christian's faith, however. To be killed isn't the worst; to lose one's relationship with God is. If you are ever in a dangerous situation, then, you can say, "They can't do any more than kill me. But for me, that's not the end, so I don't have to be afraid." The Christian's testimony is that, once having learned to love and fear God, to put God first, his other fears are dissolved.

This, then, must be the first resolution: I will fear God and no other.

I Will Accept God's Love

This resolution naturally follows the first. What begins as an acknowledgement of God's power and majesty matures into a relationship. God is powerful, that is obvious. What is not so apparent, but is the truth that God reveals to us in Christ, is that this powerful God loves us. Make that personal. God loves *me*. I will accept the fact that God has accepted *me*.

When I was a young Christian, I had considerable difficulty understanding the love of God. I had sung "Jesus Loves Me" in Sunday school, and I still think it is the most important Christian song ever written. But as I grew a little older and began wrestling with the concepts of God—His omnipotence, His omniscience, and

12

the immensity of the universe with its incomprehensible number of galaxies—I couldn't imagine how God could love me. I still can't. But I accept it.

My marriage has helped me. For over a quarter of a century, I have lived with a woman who has loved me and accepted me, and I don't understand that, either. Neither do I understand her. But I believe she loves me and she has proved she accepts me, so I have decided to enjoy both the fact of her acceptance and her.

In the same way, I receive God's love and acceptance. I can't understand all I know, but I accept it, and in that acceptance, I banish fear. "There is no fear in love. But perfect love drives out fear, because fear has to do with punishment. The one who fears is not made perfect in love" (1 John 4:18). Having experienced perfect love through Christ, the Christian soon learns he doesn't have to be afraid. "If God is for us, who can be against us? He who did not spare his own Son, but gave him up for us all—how will he not also, along with him, graciously give us all things?" (Romans 8:31, 32).

Let me return to marriage again, since it so beautifully illustrates this tension between love and fear. The husband who fears his wife or is insecure about his marriage will give way to jealousy. He excuses his abominable attitude because, he says, "I love her so much." What he is talking about isn't love, though. He cares more about himself than about her. If he loved her enough to want the best for her regardless of how that affected him, he would be incapable of jealousy. His love would drive away his jealousy and all the rest of his fears.

This, then, is the second resolution: I will accept God's love, I will return God's love, and I will not be afraid of losing it.

I Will Trust God

I will not only quote, but I will believe, Psalm 23:

> The Lord is my shepherd, I shall not be in want.
>   He makes me lie down in green pastures,
> he leads me beside quiet waters,
>   he restores my soul.
> He guides me in paths of righteousness
>   for his name's sake.
> Even though I walk
>   through the valley of the shadow of death,

I will fear no evil,
   for you are with me;
your rod and your staff,
   they comfort me.
You prepare a table before me
   in the presence of my enemies.
You anoint my head with oil;
   my cup overflows.
Surely goodness and love will follow me
   all the days of my life,
and I will dwell in the house of the Lord
   forever.

The late Joe Bayly, who was one of my favorite Christian columnists, told in his book *The Last Thing We Talk About* of the deaths of three of the Bayly children. Speaking of one of them, he recalled that someone came and talked to him, telling him of God's dealings, explaining why the death happened, offering hope beyond the grave, and so on. He talked and talked.

Bayly remained unmoved. He wished his visitor would leave.

Another friend came and just sat beside Joe. He didn't say much and he didn't ask leading questions. When Bayly said something, this friend sincerely listened, answered in a few words, prayed simply, and left. "I was moved. I was comforted. I hated to see him go."[3]

That has been my experience with the Good Shepherd. No lightning and thunder, no special revelations, no private audiences in the throne room, no lengthy explanations. Instead, steady friendship, comforting presence, and His assurance that I can trust Him to do what's best for me.

Finally, the fourth resolution.

I Will Decide to Love

"Perfect love drives out fear." God loves me with His perfect love, and that banishes my fear of Him, but there remains one step more I must take. I must love in turn—love Him who first loved me and love at least one other. This love for God and other persons drives away fear. For example, my love for my children has given this father courage I would never have had without it. There have been times when I have had to be fearless on their behalf. Love demanded it, and love made it possible.

I read a good bad example in the paper some time ago. It seems that when a young man walked out on his fiance because he couldn't cope with her blindness, she banged her head against the wall in despair. Surprisingly, the jolt to her head brought sight back to her eyes, and she could see for the first time since she lost her sight at eleven.

She called her boyfriend. He came back, and they resumed the romance and got married. He told reporters that he now feels terrible that he left her in the first place. If she were to go blind now, he said, he would stay with her.

If I had been the minister, I'm not certain I could have married them. He was a bad risk, even when he returned. I don't know what it was he felt for her in the first place, but it wasn't love. Love doesn't run; if fear drives it away, it can't be love. Perfect love casts out fear.

Paul Yonggi Cho tells of a prominent Korean political leader who learned how perfect love casts out fear. When the North Koreans attacked Seoul, the soldiers invaded quickly. Unable to escape, Mrs. Park disguised herself as an old peddler, but she was apprehended as she tried to flee to the south. The soldiers took her in for questioning and, when they looked at her soft hands, they knew she wasn't a peasant but a person of prominence. They sentenced her to be shot at dawn and threw her into a prison cell.

A young man of about twenty awakened her and marched her off to her execution. They walked several blocks. Along the way, she reviewed her active political career, first in the resistance movement against occupying Japan, then in the politics of free Korea. Her mind went back to the little church she had known as a girl. She began humming some of the hymns. One of them was "What a Friend We Have in Jesus." She realized she had never really given herself to Jesus Christ as Savior.

Summoning her courage, she took care of the matter even as she walked. She confessed herself to be a sinful woman who didn't deserve salvation, but asked for forgiveness and salvation, comparing herself to the thief on the cross.

She said that joy and peace and a sense of freedom suddenly began filling her heart, and she started to sing aloud, "All our sins and griefs to bear. What a privilege to carry, everything to God in prayer."

The soldier ordered her to shut up, but she couldn't. Besides, why should she obey him? She was going to die anyway. She told the young man that she had just given her life to her Lord and Savior Jesus Christ, and she was going to spend her last few minutes left on earth in His praise.

"Blessed assurance, Jesus is mine; oh, what a foretaste of glory divine," she sang. They arrived at the gravesite. The young man dug her grave to the accompaniment of her singing. Then as he blindfolded her, he asked if she wanted to say anything before he killed and buried her.

She told him she did. She spoke to him about her wonderful life, but said that something even more wonderful had happened to her on the way to her execution. He must have noticed the difference in her. She had been only a nominal Christian before, but now she had turned herself over completely to the Lord. She then asked if she could spend the last moments of her life praying for his soul.

She stepped into her grave, knelt, and began to pray for him. When she finished, she heard the young man crying. "I am finished. You may shoot me now," she told him. Nothing happened. She repeated herself, "I am finished praying. You may shoot."

He couldn't. He told her she reminded him of his mother praying for him. He couldn't shoot his mother. Instead, he ordered her to run away as he shot into the sky.

Mrs. Park told Pastor Cho that she had spent the rest of her life witnessing to Korean leaders concerning Jesus Christ's ability to deliver and set prisoners free. She started the first presidential prayer breakfast in Korea.[4]

When she began to love the Lord with perfect love, she banished fear.

---

[1]*Psychology Today,* February 1985, p. 16.

[2]David Schwartz, *The Magic of Thinking Big* (New York: Cornerstone Library, 1959), pp. 24, 25.

[3]Quoted in Charles R. Swindoll, *Growing Strong in the Seasons of Life* (Portland: Multnomah Press, 1983), p. 172.

[4]Paul Y. Cho, *More Than Numbers* (Waco: Word Books, 1984), pp. 73-76.

2
But That's Not Fair
Luke 1:25, 68-74; Matthew 10:16, 22, 23;
Ephesians 2:14-16

Not too long ago, I experienced a new form of prejudice, at least new to me. Several of the distinguished members of our church were riding our motorcycles in the Arizona hills and stopped for breakfast at the marina at Apache Lake. The lead riders asked the proprietor for directions to the restaurant. He pointed out that it was the building just ahead, and then none-too-tactfully suggested that he would appreciate it if we would park behind and use the back door. It was the first time since I was a child that I had been sent around to the back door. It didn't seem fair that we should be treated this way just because we were on motorcycles.

It wasn't fair. But there are many, many things in life that are unfair, aren't there? In 1978, a human skull was found in a tiger shark in Nepal Province, South Africa. A controversy about its proper burial immediately arose, because the authorities didn't know where it should rest in peace. You see, in South Africa, there are four kinds of cemeteries: one for white people, one for colored, one for Asians, and one for blacks. It is against the law to bury somebody anywhere but in the cemetery for corpses of the deceased's own color. However, when all you have is a skull, obeying the law isn't easy.

Such discrimination is unfair, isn't it?

Unfortunately, however, discriminating is what people do best. Make a list of all the causes of war and other forms of inhumanity you can think of, and at the top you have to write, "Human prejudice."

God's opinion of discrimination has perhaps been best summarized by the wise old rabbi who, when asked to explain why in the beginning God made only two people said, "That's so that nobody could ever say, 'I come from better stock than you come from.'" God's prophets thundered against social and economic prejudice, always speaking on behalf of the widowed and orphaned and downtrodden. God identified with them in their struggles by sending His Son to be born to a woman who seemed to have violated social morality, who had to flee with her husband and baby to become refugees in a foreign land, whose family then returned to a town of poor reputation (Nazareth) to struggle for a living as members of the unpopular Jewish race. In Christ's early life, God was speaking against prejudice.

He did the same in the case of John the Baptist. When John's mother Elizabeth became pregnant, she praised God: "The Lord has done this for me.... In these days he has shown his favor and taken away my disgrace among the people" (Luke 1:25). A barren woman suffered the shame of her failure to give her husband sons.

Her husband Zechariah, filled with the Holy Spirit, praised God "because he has come and has redeemed his people" who were even then objects of racial scorn in the Roman empire. Zechariah knew that somehow through the birth of his son John, salvation would rescue them "from the hand of all who hate us," so that God's people could "serve him without fear" (Luke 1:68-74).

This chapter concerns these and other forms of prejudice and what to do about them.

In This World, You Can't Expect Justice

God is just, but people aren't. Human nature quickly chooses sides and learns young how to separate the good guys from the bad guys. A psychologist showed some of his photos taken in Russia to a class of fifth and sixth graders, children of middle-class faculty and professional families. Several of the pictures showed tree-lined lanes and roads. One of the children wondered why they had trees along the road. The psychologist turned the question back to the class. "So that people won't be able to see what's going on beyond the road," was one guess. "It's to make work for prisoners," was another.

When the children were asked why we plant trees along the roads in our country, they said that they were for shade, or to keep the dust down. Even at this young age, these children were already convinced that Americans do things from good motives but Russians from bad.

When I learned of these children, my mind went back to my elementary school days. It was quite proper, even socially necessary, to hate the Germans and the "Japs." We were at war, and to hate

18

our enemies, including Germans and Japanese within our own borders, was a requirement of patriotism.

We learned the lesson so well that it took many, many years for us to get over it. When I was in college, I took my dear friend Ted Yamamori to California to spend Thanksgiving with my father and stepmother. The folks invited some other guests in, and it was only later that I learned that one of them was extremely uncomfortable. He hated all "Japs," and could hardly sit at the table with my Japanese friend. The war had been over for more than a decade.

In more recent years, I have visited both Germany and Japan (and Italy, too, for that matter), and I have tried to recall just what it was about the people in these countries that we found so heinous in those days. The people I looked upon love each other, just as we do; the husbands provide for their families and the wives take care of them, just as here; they work as we work, love as we love, laugh as we laugh, commit the same sins we do, and when they cry, they cry real tears, just like ours. But when we were at war with them, they were supposed to be different. *Patriotic prejudice* makes no sense in peacetime.

Racial prejudice, on the other hand, is always with us. In our country, its most obvious popular target is blacks, although I have lived where Hispanics and Indians and—please pardon me—"white trash" are the most cherished objects of hatred.

Let me talk about blacks for a moment. Are you aware of how they came to America in the first place? Their struggle in this hemisphere began in the West Indies in 1517. That year, the Spanish missionary Bartolome de las Casas, pitying the Indians who were languishing in the workpits of the Antillean Indies gold mines, suggested to King Charles V of Spain that he relieve the Indians of their back-breaking labors by importing blacks, so that they could do the languishing! He regretted his suggestion almost immediately, but the idea caught on and the slave trade began to flourish. Unfortunately, in almost every nation on earth, lighter is brighter and darker is for serving.

One of the most famous of all instances of extreme racial prejudice in history occurred in this century in Europe. The Nazi attempt to systematically annihilate an entire race still sickens us. Their irrational hatred of Jews was never more clearly expressed than when Dr. Goebbels said, "A Jew is for me an object of physical disgust. I vomit when I see one.... Christ could not possibly have been a Jew. I don't have to prove that scientifically. It is a fact. I treasure an ordinary prostitute above a married Jewess." So he helped kill Jews by the millions.

We don't need to say anything about *religious prejudice,* do we? All we have to do is watch the evening news to observe the latest carnage in the Middle East. There will be no peace as long as Jew hates Muslim and Muslim hates anybody who isn't Muslim. We Christians can't congratulate ourselves on being above such animosity, though. The same evening news program will undoubtedly show a clipping of the never-ending strife between Protestants and Catholics in Northern Ireland.

And I haven't said anything about *discrimination on the basis of sex or age.* There should be a law, shouldn't there, to do away with prejudice in every form? Yet, as one of our country's wisest jurists, Learned Hand, warned a group of newly naturalized citizens, "I often wonder whether we do not rest our hopes too much upon constitutions, upon laws, and upon courts. These are false hopes; believe me, these are false hopes." Many immigrants to our country have concluded with Plato's Thrasymachus (in *The Republic),* that "justice is nothing else than the interest of the stronger."

This has sounded pretty bleak so far, hasn't it? I have dwelt at length on the subject, though, in order to prepare us for Jesus' very realistic words of warning. When He sent His disciples out on their trial mission, He didn't withhold anything, but thoroughly prepared them for the inevitable. They were going out to do good in His name. People ought to appreciate them, applauding their efforts and cheering their motives, since they would heal the sick, cast out demons, and cleanse the lepers. Gratitude would not be their pay, however. Instead, Jesus cautioned, "I am sending you out like sheep among wolves. Therefore be as shrewd as snakes and as innocent as doves. . . . All men will hate you because of me, but he who stands firm to the end will be saved" (Matthew 10:16, 22). Jesus did not, and does not, promise fair treatment for His disciples. A Rodney Dangerfield among us could legitimately wail, "I get no respect."

In This World, God Works for Justice

Yet we have no reason to despair. This is still our Father's world, and He is still working in it—and always on the side of justice and mercy: "I have told you these things, so that in me you may have peace. In this world you will have trouble. But take heart! I have overcome the world" (John 16:33).

20

Here again Jesus forces us to face facts: there will be trouble. There will be something more for His disciples, however. They have the assistance of the Overcomer. The promise is repeated in 1 John 4:4: "You, dear children, are from God and have overcome them, because the one who is in you is greater than the one who is in the world." Add to these the wonderful words of Revelation 15:3:

> Great and marvelous are your deeds,
>   Lord God Almighty.
> Just and true are your ways,
>   King of the ages.

He is just and the source of justice. From Him, and from Him only, we can expect fairness. Although we might suffer at the hands of sinful humanity, through Christ we have access to the Just One: "For Christ also hath once suffered for sins, the just for the unjust, that he might bring us to God" (1 Peter 3:18, KJV). Then, when He has brought us to God, we can relax, as the Lord himself proclaims through the prophet Isaiah:

> There is no God else beside me; a just God and a Saviour; there is none beside me.
> Look unto me, and be ye saved, all the ends of the earth: for I am God, and there is none else (Isaiah 45:21, 22, KJV).

These verses summarize the case, don't they? You cannot expect justice in this sin-filled world, but you can trust that God will treat you fairly. He is just; He keeps His word; He fulfills His promises. He won't send you around to the back door.

How does God bring about justice in this unjust world?

He Is Working From Upside Down

Salvation has come into the world from above, down to us, down to all of us. As we used to sing in Sunday school,

> Jesus loves the little children,
> *All* the children of the world;
> Red and yellow, black and white,
> They are precious in His sight,
> Jesus loves the little children of the world.

The heart of the Bible's message is that "God so loved the world that he gave his one and only Son, that *whoever* believes in him shall not perish but have eternal life" (John 3:16). Nobody is excluded for any reason from this offer. This is a truth that we cannot appreciate from looking around us, but only by looking above us, where Christ is, reigning in just and merciful glory. It is through Him we are reconciled to God and to one another; there are no distinctions among His own (see 2 Corinthians 5:14-19; Galatians 3:26-29).

In undergraduate college, I was privileged to study under a brilliant Christian professor who taught us how important it is for us Christians to look upward, to let ourselves be drawn to where Christ is. He was a member of a different fellowship from mine, and in those days I could be pretty dogmatic about the absolute correctness of the opinions of my group. We could heal all the divisions in Christianity, I fervently believed, if everybody would simply start thinking the way we did.

He was of a different persuasion, however, and was not about to be swayed by his young student. Instead, he taught me. While discussing denominationalism one day, we agreed that the way believers have separated into opposing camps is sinful; we disagreed on the way to bring them together. I've never forgotten his simple words. He merely pointed out that, no matter how varied our backgrounds, as we draw closer to Christ, we grow closer to each other. He drew an equilateral triangle and wrote Christ on top, illustrating how our ascension toward the Lord brought us closer to one another and how, the closer we came to Him, the more like Him we would become and the more we would see as He sees, without prejudice but with love and acceptance.

It was a simple lesson, but one I needed then.

And now.

I recently learned another lesson about it, from a very different source. A survey was taken of eleven major symphony orchestras to learn what players in one section thought of other players. It was discovered that string instrumentalists are thought of as effeminate wimps and prima donnas; brass players are loud, beer-drinking jocks; percussionists are "insensitive, unintelligent, and hard of hearing, yet humorous and fun at parties." I was eager to learn about the woodwind section, since I used to play the clarinet. Our section, it was reported, is held in highest esteem; we lovers of the reed are described as "quiet, meticulous, and intelligent."

Of course, I thought. Then I read the next words, ". . . although somewhat egotistical."[1]

Can you believe it? All these people having such critical views of each other? Yet, when we sit in the audience and enjoy their music, we are unaware of any of these tensions. How can this be? It is because up in front of them is their conductor, and the closer they all come to the conductor's wishes, the closer musically they come to one another.

In the church and in the world, the more closely we follow the Conductor, the more we lose our prejudices. For this reason, God sent His Son, from Heaven downward (see Philippians 2:5-11), to bring us together in one body characterized by mercy and justice and mutual acceptance.

He Is Working From Outside In

Prophets, through whom God has spoken to His people, have always been outsiders, standing at the edge of society, where they can see more clearly the injustices of the people of God.

Earlier I mentioned John the Baptist. What a wonderful example he is. Born to aged parents, born into a despised race, born of a woman who had lived much of her adult life in disgrace because she was childless, John was from the beginning an outsider. And so he remained, separated by his vow to drink no wine or other fermented drink, filled by the Holy Spirit, ministering in the Jordan wilderness rather than in synagogues or the temple, subsisting on a spartan diet of locusts and wild honey. Because he owed no man anything, he could speak fearlessly. And what he said called God's people to repentance and justice.

Today's preachers have, among their other responsibilities, a prophetic ministry. God has also called us to stand apart, ultimately to rely on no one except Him, to proclaim a message of truth and righteousness, and to call people everywhere to repent and be reconciled to God and one another. Ours is the voice of the outsider, still preparing the way for the coming of the Lord to change the hearts of men and women.

He Is Working From Inside Out

Jesus came to us from outside and made His way into our society and our hearts by becoming one of us. Then, having become like us, He has made it possible for us to become like Him, a new person, reconciled and at peace with all others in Him:

> For he himself is our peace, who has made the two one and has destroyed the barrier, the dividing wall of hostility, by abolishing in his flesh the law with its commandments and regulations. His purpose was to create in himself one new man out of the two, thus making peace, and in this one body to reconcile both of them to God through the cross, by which he put to death their hostility (Ephesians 2:14-16).

His is a transforming ministry, enabling us to transcend our own propensity for prejudice. He changes us from the inside out.

A little black boy at the county fair was watching the vendor fill his balloons with helium. A red one slipped out of his hand and flew skyward. A crowd began to gather, expecting to see some more balloons released, so the vendor released a yellow one. Then the little fellow asked, "If you let a black one go, will it go up into the sky as high as the others?"

"Son," the balloon man told him, "it isn't the color but the stuff inside that makes it fly."

It isn't our color, nor our wealth, nor our heritage that makes us rise, either, but what's inside. The One who was above us came down to rescue, cleanse, and fill us with the Spirit that can lift us back up to Him. Being thus filled, we rise above prejudice, we fight against injustice, we become in every respect more and more like the One who lifts us.

What can the average Christian do, then, to make life a little easier for people in this unfair, discriminating world? We feel so helpless against such odds. Undoubtedly, all God's prophets and servants have felt this way, yet they did what they could, and the world was improved because they lived.

If we cannot do great things, perhaps we can do little things that make a difference. Let me tell you of just one. There was a schoolteacher in a shantytown near Johannesburg, South Africa, who saw something he had never seen before: a white man tipping his hat to a black woman. It seems a small thing to us, but in that strictly segregated country, it was a daring act. The woman was the schoolteacher's mother, and the man was an Anglican priest, Trevor Huddleston. Desmond Tutu, the teacher, never forgot that simple act of human kindness. Later, when Tutu was hospitalized, Huddleston visited him daily for twenty months.

Because of this man's kindness and his sterling Christian example, Desmond Tuto was inspired to leave the schoolroom for the ministry. In time, he became bishop, and then archbishop and a

Nobel Peace Prize winner for his non-violent leadership in black South Africa's struggle for justice. His courageous career began with a tip of the hat to a woman.

We started this chapter by enumerating some of the many ways in which this world is not fair. We finish with the realization that though prejudice and injustice seem to prevail, among Christians they must not be tolerated. Every Christian must become as much like Christ as possible. Though everyone else be prejudiced, the Christian must "regard no one from a worldly point of view" (2 Corinthians 5:16). Here, instead, is what we can do:

(1) Trust in the just God.

"So we say with confidence, 'The Lord is my helper; I will not be afraid. What can man do to me?'" (Hebrews 13:6).

(2) Don't expect more than the Lord promises.

He never promised that on earth we would escape suffering or discrimination.

(3) As far as possible, live without prejudice.

"Do not conform any longer to the pattern of this world, but be transformed by the renewing of your mind" (Romans 12:2).

Though others may discriminate against you because of your religion or race or sex or whatever, you will not retaliate in kind but will adopt a Christlike spirit of forgiveness and acceptance.

(4) Take seriously Christ's command: love your neighbor as yourself.

After all, that's only fair, isn't it?

---

[1]"Orchestral Dissonance," *Psychology Today,* November 1983, p. 80.

3

Pride Goeth Also Before Depression
Lamentations 3:19-26; Matthew 11:2, 3

Went to the river, couldn't get across,
Paid five dollars for an old gray hoss.
Hoss wouldn't pull so I traded for a bull.
Bull wouldn't holler so I traded for a dollar.
Dollar wouldn't pass so I threw it on the grass.
Grass wouldn't grow so I traded for a hoe.
Hoe wouldn't dig so I traded for a pig.
Pig wouldn't squeal so I traded for a wheel.
Wheel wouldn't run so I traded for a gun.
Gun wouldn't shoot so I traded for a boot.
Boot wouldn't fit so I thought I'd better quit.
So I quit.[1]

Who hasn't felt like quitting sometimes? Many times? There are days when, as in the nonsense poem above, everything seems to go wrong. When those days stretch into weeks, and then months, and maybe years, disappointment turns into discouragement and discouragement into depression. When that happens, you're in real trouble.

I don't read the Old Testament book of Lamentations too often, especially when I'm looking for a pick-me-up. Its title gives it away. It's the writer's lament over the destruction of the city of Jerusalem and over his own distressful life. He has been stricken with afflictions so severe that he feels God himself has driven him away from His presence. He's an emotional and physical wreck.

My splendor is gone
and all that I had hoped from the Lord (Lamentations 3:18).

He sounds like a defeated, depressed man.

This passage came to mind one day when I was reading the touching glimpse we are given of the final days of John the Baptist. I couldn't help wondering about his state of mind. He was in prison. King Herod threw him there for rebuking the king for his illicit liaison with his brother's wife. Such impudence is not to be tolerated, even from a prophet of God. You know John's fate: he is destined to die for his courage.

Matthew tells us that in prison, John heard of "what Christ was doing." He must have been puzzled; Jesus was not fulfilling John's expectations. So to ease his mind, John "sent his disciples to ask him, 'Are you the one who was to come, or should we expect someone else?'" (Matthew 11:2, 3). I don't want to read too much into this brief episode, but I can't help wondering whether John wasn't assessing his entire ministry—and wondering. He had staked his life on the messiahship of Jesus. He had selflessly told his disciples that the power and influence of Jesus must increase as his own decreased. But then he heard rumors of Jesus insulting the religious leaders and breaking the Sabbath and consorting with sinners, while all the time giving little or no indication that He would succeed in establishing the kingdom of God on earth. What was John to think? Had he been wrong? Had Jesus gone astray? Nothing would have been more depressing for John than to discover he had given his life in vain!

The Bible thus gives us glimpses into the darker moments of two prophets, Jeremiah (to whom Lamentations is attributed) and John, stalwarts of faith. If even such spiritual giants as these can have their downers, surely we won't escape.

The Source of My Hopelessness

To help us understand depression a little better, we need to take a few moments to think about its sources. There are several, but they have a common characteristic. All of them in one way or another are expressions of personal pride.

I Can't Get What I Want

I mentioned Rodney Dangerfield's famous line in the last chapter: "I get no respect." It's a funny line—so long as it isn't true. Nothing is more depressing, however, than to feel that nobody respects you. Nobody's pride can stand total rejection.

Maybe it isn't respect that you can't get, however, but something at least as devastating. I was deeply moved in reading Florence

Littauer's story of her two boys. Always the optimist, this attractive, intelligent, vivacious woman had married well. The wedding pictures of Florence and her prominent New York banker groom appeared in *Life* magazine. The young couple prospered in business and at home, being blessed by two beautiful daughters.

Then Florence gave birth to the apple of his father's eye— Frederick Jerome Littaur III. He was all a parent could want in a son, until he was about eight months old. Then something went desperately wrong. He began to scream fitfully. He couldn't sit up. His eyes glazed and he stopped smiling.

After running several tests, the doctor told the Littaurs that their son was hopelessly brain damaged. As kindly as he could, he advised them to put him away and forget about him. They could have another son. They were stunned and unbelieving. Surely somebody somewhere could fix him up. The doctor assured them that this was one problem neither their money nor their will power could do anything about. The baby was hopeless.

Hopeless. That was a new word in Florence Littaur's vocabulary, and she refused to accept it.

They did, however, have a second son, and the mother poured her love out on him. Then, one week after Freddie died at two years of age, she picked up her baby Larry from his nap. To her horror, she saw the same blank look, the same glazed eyes, and the same failure to respond. The doctor struggled for words. "I don't know how to say this, Florence, but I'm afraid he has the same thing."

Another futile round of hospitals. Again, there was nothing that could be done.

Florence said that life just stopped for her. She fell into a deep depression. Every *thing* she had valued before now seemed totally meaningless: money, twelve-room house, wall-to-wall carpeting, all of it. She couldn't get what she wanted most, the health and life of her sons.

Only much later, and only with the help of the Lord, was Florence able to pick up her life again. Now she has been God's blessing all over America as she shares her story of failed pride, depression, and renewal in the Lord.[2]

"I can't get what I want." Florence wanted the lives of her babies. Nothing could be more admirable than this desperate love of a mother for her handicapped sons, but she still couldn't have what she wanted. Others plunge into despair because they can't get the job they want or need, or the promotion they think they deserve, or the woman (or man) they dream of, or the thanks they have coming, or even the food they need to eat.

I Can't Keep What I Don't Want to Lose

This is saying the same thing, but with a difference. It's on my mind because of a good friend who is about to lose his farm. The 1980s haven't been kind to farmers. One Iowa man, you probably remember reading about him, went berserk over the prospect of losing the family place. He killed his wife, killed a fellow farmer, then drove to town and killed the bank president. Finally, he shot himself. He couldn't cope with losing what had been his for his entire life.

You have undoubtedly heard of Dr. Thomas Holmes's stress test. As a psychiatrist with the University of Washington School of Medicine, Dr. Holmes developed a scale to measure the relative stress induced by various changes in a person's life. He calculates that if you accumulate more than 200 points on his scale, you are a prime candidate for either physical or emotional illness. Among his items, he includes the following:

loss of a spouse	100 points
divorce (another kind of loss)	75 points
marital separation (also a loss)	65 points
jail term (loss of freedom)	63 points
death of close family member	63 points
fired at work	47 points

Is it any wonder, then, that when you sustain an important loss, you also suffer from a mild (or more severe) form of depression?

Let me add a byword of caution here. Since loss hits us with such force, we need not add the burden of guilt to our already heavy load. Do not lecture yourself with these too-frequent words of condemnation: "After all, I'm a Christian and Christians are always supposed to smile and never get discouraged." Sometimes you feel let down whether you are a Christian or not. You are merely being normal.

I Have What I Want

Surprisingly, sometimes depression comes because I have what I want. I've reached what I was after. No more goals.

30

More than one person has discovered that the two greatest tragedies in life are first, not getting what you want, and secondly, getting it. Back in the 1950s, Robert Young was involved in one of the most bitter proxy fights in our country. It seems that he wanted to own and run a railroad, so he bought himself one. It was a bitter fight, but in time, he wrested control of the New York Central from its owners. Unfortunately, after he bought it, he found out he was unable to manage it. He couldn't make the trains run on time or within budget. He got what he wanted, but one day in his Palm Beach home, he blew his head away with a twenty-gauge shotgun.

Depression is a subject I know a little something about. I'm not given to it normally, but I did experience it when I completed my doctor's degree program. For fourteen years, I had been working toward that degree. Joy and I married the week I graduated from Northwest Christian College with my first degree. She thought she had married a man who had completed his formal education. I fooled her! I went to college for ten more years.

They weren't always easy years, either. We had to struggle financially, balancing the demands of a growing family against the ever-rising costs of education. But they were fruitful years of personal growth toward a future.

Then we reached the future. The diploma for which I had labored was in my hand. The goal was accomplished. And I became depressed. Nothing seemed worthwhile. Nothing. It was not until I identified new goals and gave myself to them that I pulled out. (I can't help thinking of John the Baptist in that prison cell. He had accomplished his ministry of paving the way for Jesus. His future was uncertain. If Jesus was indeed the expected Messiah, there was little more for John to do. Did he feel as I felt when my longtime goal was achieved?)

This is the essence of the mid-life crisis, isn't it? Youth has a future, makes plans, sees visions, dreams dreams. Middle age settles down. It has accumulated some possessions, is fairly satisfied, isn't going anywhere, isn't living toward any purpose—and wonders why the joy has gone out of life. If that's where you are, the problem may well be that you've got what you wanted.

I can't speak of the retirement years from personal experience, but as a minister, I've often heard the blues from many people who've reached this plateau. Retirees, your problem may originate in the fact that you've got what you wanted. For years, you planned for retirement—but not beyond. Now you have what you wanted, and it isn't as good as you thought it would be. So you've given up. Too much drinking. Too much eating. Too much time on your hands. Too much recreation. No new goals, nothing to sacrifice for, nothing for which to get up early or work late. You feel proud of what you were, but not of what you are.

We all need somebody to need us, a cause to depend on us, to call out the best from us. The alternative is depression.

I Refuse to Face the Facts

I need to be rather blunt here. Sometimes depression comes because I refuse to face the facts. Crises and losses come to all of us; we cannot make them disappear by refusing to admit that they've happened. Let me use divorce as the example. He's left. She's leaving. What is your immediate reaction? Very often, it is one of denial. "Oh no, it can't be." "This is just temporary. He's coming back. She's going to return. It's going to be as it was before, only better. I'm going to make it better."

But it doesn't get better.

This happens with dying, doesn't it? You learn you have a terminal illness. "No, it's not happening to me. I won't accept it. I won't tolerate it." But the disease won't be willed away.

You can add more: impending financial disaster, problems with the children, a loved one's addiction. You are too proud to face facts. And depression gets you.

Can you stand to hear about just one more source of depression—without becoming depressed? This is a big one.

I Haven't Amounted to Much

This also generally afflicts us in the middle and later years, although young people aren't immune. It hits when we take stock and find that huge, gaping chasm between our aspirations and our achievements. It's what Winston Churchill expressed when, as an old man celebrating his birthday, he said to his daughters, "I have achieved a great deal to achieve nothing in the end." Robert Louis Stevenson, author of such popular books as *Treasure Island* and *Kidnapped,* wrote his own epitaph: "Here lies one who meant well, who tried a little, and failed much." Cecil Rhodes, who opened up South Africa to the white man, said as he lay dying, "So little done, so much to do." I felt a touch of this melancholy when at thirty-five I had to face the fact that my time would run out before my dreams would be realized.

Enough of the reasons. I like Philip Toynbee's approach. Having examined his own depression for its causes and ways to get rid of them, he began searching for purposes in it that he could fulfill. He concluded that "depression is often a sign, whether human or divine, that the life of the victim needs to be drastically changed; that acts of genuine contrition are called for. . . ."[2] This call for a change takes us back to Lamentations, where we learn that the writer has found the solution.

The Source of My Hope

Having remembered his affliction and bitterness (Lamentations 3:1-20), Jeremiah abruptly switched in verse 21: "Yet this I call to mind." He is taking control of his mind, deliberately recalling positive things. (Sometimes affirmations don't voluntarily come. Make them come!)

> Yet this I call to mind
> and therefore I have hope. [Then he mentions the source.]
> Because of the Lord's great love we are not consumed,
> for his compassions never fail.

Notice: He doesn't have great miracles or marvels in mind at all, but everyday occurrences.

> They are new every morning;
> great is your faithfulness (Lamentations 3:21-23)

What's new every morning? Well, in the first place, *morning* is new every morning. Start there. Greet the day. Remember, there are two ways to begin. Either, "Good morning, Lord." Or, "Good Lord, morning!" It's a good day. The sun is shining. Or the rain is falling. Or the wind is blowing—but it's a new day and you can make a new beginning.

Then get out of bed. Stop right here. Did you give thanks for that? I have a friend who can't get up unaided, who will never be able to, this side of Heaven. You can, so what are you complaining about? Put your feet on the floor. Okay, so when you do that you feel your arthritis. Give thanks for it. You can *feel!* My friend can't put his feet on the floor—and if he could, he still couldn't *feel* the floor.

Are you beginning to get my point?

A student put himself through four years of college by taking care of a paraplegic fellow student. He was paid an allowance to be his roommate and assist him in getting to his classes. At the commencement exercises, all the graduates stood to applaud their handicapped classmate. Many years later, his roommate said that the finest thing that had ever happened to him was the privilege of living with his paraplegic friend. He said that he never had any difficulties after that without remembering how hard it was for his roommate to do anything at all. Yet he never complained; he just did what he had to do, even when it hurt.[4]

Think of the little things we have for which to be grateful. Look at your hand, for example. What a mechanical marvel. Do you thank God for it? No, you take it for granted, just as I do. Like me, do you grumble about your bifocals? Or do you thank God you can see? Like me, do you complain because you are deaf in one ear? Or do you thank God the other one works? Are you upset because somebody has hurt your feelings? Or do you thank the Lord for your faithful friends who stand by you, even when you aren't worthy of their loyalty?

Little things. Like a good hot bath, surely one of the greatest of all luxuries. Like the touch of somebody who loves you. Like breathing in and breathing out on your own.

If you define satisfaction in terms of the number or quality of ego-satisfying status symbols you have accumulated (a Mercedes Benz, a twelve-room house, a cottage in the mountains) or would like to, your pride is preparing you for a fall. But if you learn to find happiness in the laughter of a child, the listening ear of a friend, in the silent presence of a treasured companion, in the privilege of worship, in the sweet scent of a rose, then you will appreciate the fact that in your life, "God's compassions never fail," and joy, not depression, will be your lot in life, for these compassions are new every morning—even when things go wrong.

You may remember the famous actor Lionel Barrymore. When he broke his hip in 1936, with a fracture that never healed, most of his contemporaries thought his acting career was over. To the contrary. For the next eighteen years, always in pain, Mr. Barrymore played dozens of roles—in his wheelchair. Critics think he was better after his setback than before.

> The Lord is my portion;
>   therefore I will wait for him (Lamentations 3:24).

For a while, it looked as if one of the world's greatest preachers in his time would not be allowed to preach. G. Campbell Morgan was one of 150 young men seeking admission to the Wesleyan ministry in 1888. Having passed his doctrinal examinations, he then had to preach to a panel of ministerial judges and an audience of a few dozen—in an auditorium that would seat over 1,000. Then he had to wait two weeks to learn the judges' verdict. Of the 150 candidates, 105 were rejected. Morgan was among them.

According to Jill Morgan, his daughter-in-law, Morgan wired his father a one-word message: "Rejected." His father quickly wired him back, "Rejected on earth. Accepted in heaven. Dad."

Morgan began there to trust the truth of this Scripture, "The Lord is good to those whose hope is in him" (Lamentations 3:25). In time, Morgan proved his critics wrong and, in the power of the Lord, proclaimed His Word to thousands every week.

Just a few weeks after the roof collapsed during the construction of our new church building (severely injuring four workers and wreaking havoc with the schedule), dear friends in Oregon sent me a picture. There was no note, but none was needed. They knew I would interpret the gift correctly, because it's about home.

It depicts the Oregon coastline. The skies are cloudy and gray; a storm has just passed, and the breakers are still pounding against the beach, smoothing out the sand with their powerful thrusts. On a cliff overlooking the beach is a lighthouse, but it is not the source of the picture's light. Instead, the lighthouse itself is brightened by light from the sun. Yet the sun doesn't show itself in the picture; instead, its rays penetrate the clouds enough to reflect off the white wall of the lighthouse.

Beneath the picture is this apt quotation, Romans 8:38, 39 (King James Version): "Neither ... height, nor depth, nor any other creature, shall be able to separate us from the love of God, which is in Christ Jesus our Lord." Yes, "the Lord *is* good to those whose hope is in him ..." because "we know that in all things God works for the good of those who love him, who have been called according to his purpose" (Romans 8:28).

So you may be down for a while. It may be cloudy and stormy, and the roof may even fall in on you, but "blessed are those whose hope is in the Lord." The Sun (Son) still shines, even through the clouds.

I don't do this very often. In fact, I can't recall that I ever did it before, but last fall I had a little period of discouragement and I uncharacteristically scribbled some thoughts about my feelings, and I filed them. I found them as I was preparing this chapter. I had just returned from a meeting in Cincinnati, Ohio. On the way back home, I spent four days in the St. Louis area, preaching for the Florissant Christian Church. While there, I went to a Christian bookstore and picked up Charles Swindoll's *Growing Strong in the Seasons of Life*. It was just what I needed to read at the time. "Superb, definitely major league stuff," I wrote of it—and felt even more discouraged. How I'd like to be able to write as well as he does!

When I returned to Arizona, I purchased three more copies to give as gifts. While in the bookstore, I couldn't help noticing that none of my books was displayed as prominently as Swindoll's.

That's when I began writing. "Discouraging period," I said to myself. "People leaving." I was referring to the fact that six months earlier, we had sold our church building and had begun camping in a high school auditorium while awaiting the construction of our new one. Conditions weren't the best, and some of our members had left to seek greater comfort elsewhere. As a pastor, I was taking these losses personally. "What more could I have done, where did I go wrong?" I was asking myself. So I wrote, "People leaving. Attendance down."

Then, "Building delayed again. And again." (This was even before the roof collapsed.)

Then I penned some words about Charles Wingfield, the Florissant minister. "How I admire him. Tenacity, courage, pastoral care, six beautiful kids (two at home) heading for some form of Christian ministry." It was inspiring for me to be with him, yet I couldn't help feeling a little inferior. I've known him for years and have always admired his and his wife's genuine love of the Lord and Christian example.

"Down. I'm down," I wrote. It was the truth. As I've already told you, I don't feel this way often, but it was a low point for me. I guess I was feeling the stress more than I had wanted to admit.

But then I added, "Yet I will be faithful."

That's the line I don't mind sharing. In spite of my emotions in those days, I determined to carry on my obligations and be steadfast in my service.

What is it that God expects of us in our down times? He certainly doesn't require that we lie: "Everything's fine, everything is always fine." No, sometimes it isn't.

He doesn't want our pretending. He wants our faithfulness. He asks us to hang in there. If you're a parent, you understand this. Sometimes you get so tired of being a parent, you wonder whether you can go on. But the kids won't go away. What do you do? You hang in there. You remain faithful.

So that's what I wrote. My next line: "The peace of God came over me as I was putting the finishing touches on the morning sermon." And then in parentheses, "Sinus draining, allergies, feel yukky." That was my condition: I felt peaceful and yukky.

Then I wrote, "God will prevail."

As a P.S., I added sometime later, "That Sunday we began our two services. Attendance back up to equal with last year's average. Holding." It kept climbing.

I've told you this little story because it's my personal experience with these verses:

> The Lord is good to those whose hope is in him,
>   to the one who seeks him;
> it is good to wait quietly
>   for the salvation of the Lord (Lamentations 3:25, 26).

While my attention was absorbed by own feelings (and what is this absorption but yet another form of pride?), darkness prevailed; when I made up my mind to be faithful and to trust God, the joy of service returned. Then I could sing, "It is well, it is well with my soul."

"The Lord *is* good to those whose hope is in him. . . ."

---

[1]"Went to the River," *The World Treasury of Children's Literature,* Clifton Fadiman, ed. (Boston and Toronto: Little, Brown and Company, 1984), p. 53.

[2]Florence Littauer, *Blow Away the Black Clouds* (Eugene, Oregon: Harvest House, 1979), pp. 4, 5.

[3]*Part of a Journey* (London: William Collins Sons & Co., Ltd., 1908), p. 13.

[4]John Killinger, *For God's Sake Be Human* (Waco: Word Books, 1970), p. 138.

4
Learning to Live Now
Matthew 4:18-22, 16:24; 2 Corinthians 6:1, 2

In New Testament drama, some characters emerge for a moment, play their bit parts, and then are seen no more. There's the rich young ruler, bursting with spiritual ambition and demanding to know what worthy things he can do to secure his eternal destiny, and then, when he receives an unexpected answer, fading from the scene, never to appear again (Matthew 19).

Then there's Governor Felix, who dismisses the apostle Paul with a peremptory "That's enough for now! You may leave. When I find it convenient, I will send for you." It's never convenient enough, apparently. He does send for Paul some more, but not because he wants to hear what the apostle has to say. He is after a bribe, not what Paul has to offer: lessons on "righteousness, self-control and the judgment to come." So Felix, too, walks off the Biblical stage (Acts 24).

His successor, Governor Festus, is at least less blase than Felix. In an outburst, he scolds the evangelistic Paul: "You are out of your mind, Paul! Your great learning is driving you insane!" At his side is King Agrippa, astonished that Paul could be so presumptuous as to try to convert him. "Do you think that in such a short time you can persuade me to be a Christian?" (Acts 26).

In every case, these men display an attitude of resistance to the call of the Lord. Their moment of opportunity comes and goes, and they fail to take advantage of it. They could mutter with T. S. Eliot's ineffectual J. Alfred Prufrock, "I have seen the moment of my greatness flicker, / and in short I was afraid."

Afraid or not, they do not seize the moment.

Contrast these bit players, if you please, with the cast of starring disciples Jesus calls from their fishing nets (Matthew 4:18-22). "Come, follow me," He urges them. Immediately they obey Him. They sense their moment of opportunity—and in short, they aren't afraid. They do what the apostle Paul later urges others to do:

As God's fellow workers we urge you not to receive God's grace in vain. For he says,

"In the time of my favor I heard you,
and in the day of salvation I helped you."

I tell you, now is the time of God's favor, now is the day of salvation (2 Corinthians 6:1, 2).

These verses are often quoted out of context. Unlike most Scriptures, they really can stand alone. The stark fact is, we have no other time but now, no other day but today. We dare not live in the past, and we cannot live in the future. This alone is the day of opportunity for us, the moment for accepting God's favor, the time for entering into a saving relationship with the Lord.

Although they can stand alone, however, these verses are enriched when one reads the preceding few verses. Paul has just been arguing that "if anyone is in Christ, he is a new creation; the old has gone, the new has come!" (2 Corinthians 5:17). God has done everything necessary to make it possible for us to have new life. In Christ, He has made us new creatures (Christians) living in a new and healthful environment (the church). Here Paul urges Christians to take advantage of God's grace, making the most of it. Blessed indeed are those Christians who do, without ever again allowing the defeatist attitudes of their pre-Christian days to defeat them.

They live in the spirit of Robert Lewis Stevenson. As he lay dying in Samoa, a missionary wrote that he would like to talk to him "as to one in danger of dying." Stevenson answered that he would be willing to see him, provided he was ready to talk instead to him about the dangers of living!

Of all the dangers, this is probably the greatest: to miss the opportunities that God sends our way—for salvation, for ministry, for fulfillment, for glorifying God, for joy unspeakable.

What, then, must we do?

Open Your Eyes and Your Ears

Open my eyes, that I may see
Glimpses of truth Thou hast for me;
Place in my hands the wonderful key
That shall unclasp, and set me free.

It's a beautiful old hymn and a timely prayer, isn't it? Our problem is not that God has hidden His truth for us or that He has withheld opportunities from us. The Lord could ask of us as much as of the Pharisees, "Do you have eyes but fail to see, and ears but fail to hear?" (Mark 8:18).

Vachel Lindsay's poem says it better than I can:

Within the town of Buffalo
Are prosy men with leaden eyes.
Like ants they worry to and fro,
(Important men, in Buffalo).
But only twenty miles away
A deathless glory is at play,
Niagara, Niagara.

The women buy their lace and cry,
"Oh, such a delicate design!"
And over ostrich feathers sigh
At counters there in Buffalo.
The children haunt the trinket shops,
They buy false faces, bells and tops.
Forgetting great Niagara.

There is even more to the story than Lindsay laments. He regrets the busy-ness of "important" men and preoccupied women and unaware children who have time for everything but appreciation of the majesty of Niagara Falls. Even he misses something, though, that engineers beheld in the cascading waters. They saw untapped power, and they harnessed it to provide light and heat for homes and businesses far from the river.

As the story has come down to us, a tired and discouraged Edward L. Doheny was loitering in a hotel lobby one day, wondering how he could find the money to get back to Mexico to continue his prospecting for gold, when a rickety wagon rumbled by carrying a load of black, tarry dirt. There was something strangely familiar to Doheny about that dirt, so he rushed out to have a closer look. He asked the wagon driver where it had come from. Told that the driver had got it out by Westlake Park, Doheny caught the next trolly out there, where he found dirt tarrier and greasier than what he had seen on the wagon.

During the next few days, the prospector rushed to get permission to drill for oil on the property. When he did, he struck oil thirty feet below the surface. He and the owners of the land became

41

fabulously wealthy—because one man saw possibilities where others saw nothing but dirt.

Opportunity certainly doesn't always strike like this, but it never strikes for the person with eyes that don't see. The moral is obvious. Open your eyes and ears to what lies all around you.

When Jesus walked the Galilean trails, most of His countrymen were preoccupied with their affairs. Only a few like Peter and Andrew and James and John looked at Him with eyes that could see and listened with ears that heard. They seized their moment and, in short, they weren't afraid.

Order Your Priorities

Here's the big obstacle, isn't it? We act according to our priorities. These four fishermen *immediately* accepted Jesus' invitation. They had a higher priority than catching fish.

There was an opportune moment in the early history of America's dealings with the Soviet Union that was missed because one of the key players didn't keep his mind on his country's priorities. In April of 1917, while Allen Dulles was serving as a duty officer at the American legation in Berne, Switzerland, he had a date with a girl one evening. It was so important to him that the time with her could not be preempted, even for an appointment with someone named V. I. Lenin. His request to see Dulles having been rebuffed, Lenin left the next day for Russia, where he immediately began peace negotiations with the Germans, who were at war with the West. It was later learned that Lenin, who admired United States President Woodrow Wilson, had wanted to establish an American contact. But Dulles was too busy to have an appointment with the future leader of Communist Russia. He had a date with a girl.

You can't help wondering whether American-Russian relations might not have got off to a better start if Dulles had had a different set of priorities that night in 1917.

More than half a century earlier, another American was ordering his priorities, and his values would profoundly affect the future of his country. Long before Abraham Lincoln entered the White House, he had made up his mind on the morality of the slavery issue and was urging his countrymen to act.

You say slavery is wrong; but don't you constantly argue that this is not the right place to oppose it? You say it must not be opposed in the free states, because slavery is not there; it must not be opposed in the slave

42

states, because it is there; it must not be opposed in politics, because that will make a fuss; it must not be opposed in the pulpit, because it is not religion. Then where is the place to oppose it? There is no suitable place to oppose it.[1]

Since Lincoln could not find an acceptable time and place, he made a place and he created a time and he took advantage of his opportunities, and he opposed slavery to its death. He could set the slaves free because first of all he had ordered his own priorities.

Priorities have to do with what you want and when you want it. If you are like me, you are often crippled by wanting to do everything at once. You confuse what is urgent with what is important. You fail to grasp at once-in-a-lifetime opportunities because you are too tied up with secondary concerns.

You and I are more like Lucy (in the *Peanuts* comic strip) than we want to admit. She's in the outfield when a high fly ball is hit right to her. It drops to the ground untouched. She makes no move to catch it. Her apoplectic manager, Charlie Brown, angrily rushes out to demand an explanation. Why didn't she catch the ball? He points out that she didn't even have to take a step but just hold out her glove. Lucy's ready for him. She calmly tells him that she was having her quiet time.

Undoubtedly, Charlie Brown approved of a daily quiet time, but not during a ball game when you're playing outfielder. Her priorities are all wrong, or at least her timing is.

Let's get serious about this. James says it best (in James 4:13-17):

> Now listen, you who say, "Today or tomorrow we will go to this or that city, spend a year there, carry on business and make money." Why, you do not even know what will happen tomorrow. What is your life? You are a mist that appears for a little while and then vanishes. Instead, you ought to say, "If it is the Lord's will, we will live and do this or that." As it is, you boast and brag. All such boasting is evil. *Anyone, then, who knows the good he ought to do and doesn't do it, sins.*

This is the crux of the matter, then, isn't it? Today is all we have. The only opportunity we can be certain we shall have is the one we have right now. Wise is the person who has so ordered his life that he knows what is the most important activity for him at the given moment. He gives priority attention to priority matters.

And this is the highest priority of all:

Accept the Lord

Hear the Word of the Lord again: "I tell you, now is the time of God's favor, now is the day of salvation." Paul is writing to the Corinthians—and through them to us. A new day has arrived. The supreme opportunity is at hand: God is reaching out to take you into His embrace. You must respond, and respond now, because nothing else is finally settled in your life until this is.

Peter put it a little differently in his sermon in Jerusalem: "Repent, then, and turn to God, so that your sins may be wiped out, that times of refreshing may come from the Lord" (Acts 3:19). There is no "refreshing," no "peace that passes understanding," until you are safe in the arms of God.

Don't hesitate. You know that old adage, "He who hesitates is lost." The saying remains current because so many people have learned, often to their dismay, how true it is. One such person was Queen Ankhesenamen, widow of the famous Tutankhamen ("King Tut") of ancient Egypt. When he died, the young queen was only seventeen or eighteen years old. She immediately began scheming to save her throne, having a bare two months, the required lapse of time between his death and royal entombment, to find herself a new partner.

In the preceding two or three reigns, there had been intermarrying between the royalty of Egypt and certain Asian regimes. From among these, the young queen chose to write to the king of the Hittites: "My husband is dead and I am told that you have grown-up sons. Send me one of them, and I will make him my husband, and he shall be king over Egypt."

The Hittite king was uncertain. He called his counselors and talked the matter over with them. And talked. Time passed. Finally, he sent a reply asking the whereabouts of the dead king's son.

It took fourteen days for messengers to go from one country to the other. Ankhesenamen became more anxious. She quickly sent back her reply: "Why should I deceive you? I have no son, and my husband is dead. Send me a son of yours and I will make him king."

The Hittite king finally agreed to dispatch a son to Egypt, but by then he was too late. His moment of opportunity had passed. That's the last we know of the fate of the young widow and her potential co-ruler.[2] The Hittite king had seen his moment of greatness die, because in short, he was afraid.

Our concern here, though, is not with ancient history but with the present moment, yours and mine. The gospel has an urgency about it. The good news about salvation in Jesus Christ is a life and death matter for us. The tattered men who carry their Repent-before-it's-too-late signs to city streetcorners may cause the sophisticated to scoff, but their scoffing doesn't make the signs' message any the less true.

It's Christ's message, after all. "Repent, for the kingdom of heaven is near" was the sermon with which He commenced His ministry (Matthew 4:17), and His church preaches it still. In Him, we find the opportunity for overcoming our lower appetites, our baser instincts, our stifling mediocrity, our intellectual confusion, our moral cowardice. In Him, our hunger for God is satisfied; in Him, our will to achieve finds something worth striving for. In Him, we ascend unto the heights on which God wants us to live. It is imperative, then, that we accept Him as Lord and Savior.

Accept the Lord's Guidance

If He is Lord, then it behooves us to follow Him.

Do not confuse this willingness to obey His directives with a passive "I'm waiting to see what the Lord has in mind" mentality. On the most important matters, you already know what He has in mind. He has called you to discipleship and ministry. You can serve Him. Recall James again: "Anyone, then, who knows the good he ought to do and doesn't do it, sins." Don't fret over what you don't know. Do the things you know you are supposed to do. That's enough for now.

There comes the moment, after you have sung the hymns and heard the sermons and given your offerings and prayed your prayers, that you must arise, dust off your knees, and get on with the work at hand. "If anyone would come after me, he must deny himself and take up his cross and follow me" (Matthew 16:24).

Members of our congregation in Mesa receive this reminder every time they enter our sanctuary to worship. There against the wall, up behind the choir, just to the right of the baptistry, is a cross. It's a little unusual, however, because this cross is not upright. Instead, it is lying down. One of our members pointed out the first Sunday we met in the building that the cross was in exactly the right position for bearing. An upright cross recalls Jesus' supreme sacrifice on Golgatha. It's an appropriate symbol of the Christian faith.

The cross above the chancel area in our building, however, has at least two meanings. It is Christ's cross, but as it reclines there, it points to the arch above our baptismal pool. In natural lighting, the arch looks like an empty tomb. Just above the arch is a skylight, letting the light from heaven shine down upon the pool and the baptismal candidate. The cluster of symbols taken together indicate that Christ has accomplished His redemptive work on the cross once for all; He has descended from the cross, to suffer there no more. Nor is He in the tomb; He has risen, as He said. He is alive and triumphant, and His life is "the true light that gives light to every man . . ." (John 1:9).

It is not only Christ's cross, however; it is also ours. It waits in readiness for us to take it up and follow Jesus. As we unite with Him by baptism in His death and His resurrection to new life (Romans 6), so will we be united with Him in bearing a cross of voluntary obedience to the will of God.

The Lord says, "Come, follow me," and we follow.

With God, it's often now or never. I need to ask you right now—have you accepted Christ as your Lord? Is it well with your soul? Are you right now in harmony with God's will? That is, are you doing now, right now, what you know He wants you to be doing? Or are you still planning to get around to it someday, or content to be merely praying about it? If you are not committed to doing His will right now, to what are you giving yourself? Is it really more important to you than the will of God?

Will you make yourself this promise? Will you start following Him wherever He leads you? I made that promise years ago, and God has led me all over the world, and into the most exciting and demanding kinds of ministry, including preaching, teaching, music directing, writing, building construction, and a variety of other unexpected opportunities. When you tell Him yes, He'll keep you—if you'll pardon this wonderful cliche—growing and glowing!

"I tell you, now is the time of God's favor, now is the day of salvation."

---

[1] Carl Sandberg, *Abraham Lincoln: the Prairie Years,* Abridged ed. in one volume (New York: Harcourt, Brace, and World, Inc., 1929), p. 402.

[2] Howard Carter, *The Tomb of Tutankhamen* (Excalibur Books, E. P. Dutton, Publisher, 1972, printed in Japan; copyright 1954 by Phyllis J. Walker), pp. 11, 12.

5

In the End, Only the Generous Win
Matthew 19:16-30, 2 Corinthians 9:6-11

The rich young ruler is one person in the New Testament with whom it is easy for us to identify. There are superficial differences, of course. He was rich and a leader of his people; most of us consider ourselves relatively poor and unknown. In more important ways, however, we can see ourselves in him.

In the early stage of your Christian growth, didn't you, too, want to do everything possible to insure that you would live forever with the Lord? His question was mine: "Teacher, what good thing must I do to get eternal life?" Like him, weren't you trying to keep all the commandments? (All except the one about loving your neighbor as yourself. The Lord didn't have *your* neighbors in mind, surely!) And like him, wouldn't you have walked away in sorrow if the Lord had demanded that you give away everything you owned? That seems to be asking too much. You didn't possess as much as the rich young ruler, but what little you had was as important to you as his great wealth was to him. Not only would you and I have had great difficulty parting with our meager belongings, we could not have comprehended why we needed to.

That was then. Times have changed, and so have you and I. Now that we have enjoyed some years of friendship with Jesus (it has been four decades for me), we can understand His answer to the young man's request. We can also understand why the New Testament talks so much about our management of our money and possessions. Until we can claim victory in the Lord's name over our possessions, instead of allowing ourselves to be enslaved by them, we cannot follow Jesus wholeheartedly and cannot enter fully into a free and joyful life. Jesus spoke the undebatable truth when He said, "Where your treasure is, there your heart will be also" (Matthew 6:21).

The apostle Paul offers some of the best advice we can find on this subject of money management in 2 Corinthians 9:6-11. You'll

47

notice immediately that he treats money as a means to an end and never the end in itself. Money is for giving, for accomplishing "every good work." His approach is as far as possible from what C. Wright Mills (in *The Power Elite*) has satirically cited as the American standard:

> Of all the possible values of human society, one and one only is the truly sovereign, truly universal, truly sound, truly and completely acceptable goal of man in America. That goal is money, and let there be no sour grapes about it from the losers.[1]

This perversion of money's purpose is not peculiarly American, however. Aristotle Onassis, the Greek shipping magnate and late husband of Jacqueline Kennedy Onassis, offered his opinion that "it's the people with money who are the royalty now." At the time he offered this commonplace, his estimated net worth was half a billion dollars. Somebody told me the other day that there's a new bumper sticker that announces, "In the end, the one with the most toys wins." By that standard, Onassis was a big winner, and the monetarily poor apostle Paul was a loser.

But the Bible consistently presents the rest of the story. Now that I have lived all these years with Christ, I'll bet my life on the Bible rather than on Onassis.

If You Will Give Generously . . .

According to Paul, in the end, the one who has *given* most generously is the big winner. "Remember this: Whoever sows sparingly will also reap sparingly, and whoever sows generously will also reap generously" (2 Corinthians 9:6). I always couple this verse with another, Acts 2:46 in the Revised Standard Version, which reports that the first Christians went to the temple daily and broke bread together in each other's homes "with glad and generous hearts. . . ." Of course. Gladness and generosity are inseparable. You can't have one without the other. You've never known a generous person, have you, who was unhappy? Nor a happy person who was stingy?

Many years ago, I learned of a very successful businessman in Mississippi who, while driving on an out-of-town trip, felt his arms and legs go numb. His companions took him to a hospital, where the doctors could find nothing physically wrong with him. Instead, they guessed he was emotionally paralyzed. Weeks followed with no improvement. Then one day, after driving around the block many times, he finally went inside his wife's church to talk to her pastor. He confessed that he had been running away from God for years. The minister told him he needed to surrender to the Lord—that his health depended on it. Right then the man surrendered, but the pastor wisely suggested he pay more than lip service for his health, so the man confessed with his money, drawing up a contract to support Christian causes then and in the future.[2]

The pastor realized something that clear back in the Reformation era Martin Luther was teaching. "Man needs two conversions," he said, "the first of his heart and the second of his pocketbook."

For twenty years, I have kept a clipping in my files that I took from the paper of the First Christian Church in Johnson City, Tennessee. It's a report by Dr. Hugh McKean of Thailand about a church there that was composed of tithers. All the 400 members tithed, he said. On an income of twenty cents a week plus rice, they gave ten percent to the church. Because of their tithing, they had more money for Christian work than any other church in Thailand. They paid their own minister and sent two missionaries and their families to proclaim the gospel elsewhere. In addition, they took care of unfortunates of every kind. Most impressive to me, though, was the fact that all the members were lepers.

When I ran across that clipping again in 1981, I couldn't help contrasting it with a report I read on that year's contributions published by the Internal Revenue Service. IRS reported, unsurprisingly, that Americans who earn the most contribute the smallest percentage of their income to charity. Those who that year had earned $4,000 to $6,000 donated an average of $425, while those earning $30,000 to $50,000 contributed $869. They made ten times the earnings, but gave only two times as much.

It's a phenomenon I've often observed. A sage friend pointed out to me that the reason that the rich have so much money is that they keep it. They aren't generous. According to the wisdom of the world, then, they win.

But God keeps score differently. He likes generosity.

If You Will Give Decisively . . .

"Each man should give what he has decided in his heart to give" (2 Corinthians 9:7). Giving is a voluntary act of a free agent. Nobody, even the Lord, forces generosity. Each person makes the decision for himself.

Charles Stewart Mott of Flint, Michigan, spent his early working days as president of the Weston-Mott Company, manufacturing wheel bearings and axles. When General Motors bought him out, the larger company made him a director and in the process the largest single stockholder of the corporation. In 1963, Mott established a nonprofit foundation with 1,826,421 shares of his GM stock (worth at the time $128 million). That still wasn't all of his worth. When someone asked him how much he was worth, the philanthropist answered that it doesn't matter. As far as Mott was concerned, all that matters is what a man does with his worth. Only he can make that decision.

Some figures were published a few years ago showing how the average American decided to spend his money. The precise numbers may have changed, but the American standard of values hasn't varied much over the years. According to this report, for every dollar we give for church, charity, and education combined, we spend a dollar and a half for tobacco, nearly two dollars for alcohol, almost four dollars for personal recreation, and nine dollars preparing for future war. These figures indicate what Mr. Joe American has decided is most important in his life. He lives for today instead of tomorrow, and for himself instead of for others.

His Biblical prototype is Isaac's son Esau, who offers a good symbol of an all-too-typical approach to decision-making regarding possessions. Esau's most important asset was his birthright, which granted him all the privileges of a firstborn son. He appears on the pages of Genesis (chapter 25) as a man's man, a happy-go-lucky outdoorsman, the pride of his father. He was also impetuous, undisciplined, and shortsighted in his values. For the price of a mere meal, he squandered all the benefits (and attending responsibilities) of his birthright. When the future advantages of his birthright were compared with the tantalizing smell of that hot soup—and Esau was very hungry—he threw away his future for his immediate gratification.

You can protest that Jacob tricked him, but your argument is weak. Jacob's deceit was indefensible, but the decision lay only with Esau, and he chose foolishly.

Similarly, only you and I can decide what is of ultimate value to us; we alone are responsible for the management of our possessions. Nobody can force us to be either generous or foolish. The choice is ours.

If You Will Give Cheerfully . . .

"Not reluctantly or under compulsion, for God loves a cheerful giver" (2 Corinthians 9:7).

I don't know a single unhappy tither. One man said that the reason for his cheerfulness was not only in the fact that he and his wife never lacked for anything they needed after they began tithing. More importantly, it was because their tithing had liberated them from anxiety and calculation. They began really to trust God and not their own cleverness to provide for their needs, and He never failed them. Many of us tithers could give the same testimony.

Several years ago, I was the minister of a church that had a tradition of taking a special Christmas offering for members of the staff. The chairman of the board sent a letter to the congregation to invite their participation. One member sent the letter back to the chairman with this angry note penned at the bottom: "I read this money appeal with disgust and dismay. In these critical days of unemployment and inflation that you want to give more money to the ministers whom [sic] I feel are well paid now is just a total shock to our family. I think this money could be much more useful to the unemployed or others in economical distress. I suggest you have second thoughts on this gesture [sic] as it certainly affects our thinking about monetary support to the church."

What strikes us immediately about this letter is how angry the writer has allowed himself to become over something that was not required of him. Nobody was demanding anything from him. The chairman's appeal was for voluntary contributions from those who wished to participate. No record was kept of the donors, and no pressure was placed on anyone. It was to be a free-will offering from people who wanted to give this extra one-time gift. Our angry correspondent actually made a pretty good case, but he nullified it by his over-reaction. No one could accuse this man of being a cheerful giver. It is apparent that generosity was not his norm in giving.

The letter, which was, of course, anonymous, reminded me of that old quip, "It has been discovered that in giving till it hurts, some people are extremely sensitive to pain." Many years ago, Billy Graham added his own observation that if your church is overemphasizing finances, "it is probably because its members have failed to give God His share." He added something that I have observed for many years now, that if a person is giving God what belongs to Him, he will not complain about demands for money. "It's usually

51

the fellow who is in debt to God who gripes when the preacher or the Bible School teacher mentions money."

I have often observed that I can tell which members of a church board are tithers, although I have never looked at the church books to find out. I simply pay attention to how they vote on financial matters. The consistent negative votes do not come from the tithers. Those who have decided to put God first in their management of money and who have thereby learned generosity are cheerful in their giving and optimistic in their planning of the church's program.

They have learned to count on God's blessings.

Then God Will Return to You Abundantly ...

"And God is able to make all grace *abound* to you, so that in all things at all times, having all that you need, you will *abound* in every good work" (2 Corinthians 9:8).

In this verse, Paul is leaning heavily on the words of Malachi,

> "Bring the whole tithe into the storehouse, that there may be food in my house. Test me in this," says the Lord Almighty, "and see if I will not throw open the floodgates of heaven and pour out so much blessing that you will not have room enough for it" (Malachi 3:10).

Luke picks up this same theme in his Gospel as he quotes Jesus:

> Give, and it will be given to you. A good measure, pressed down, shaken together and running over, will be poured into your lap. For with the measure you use, it will be measured to you (Luke 6:38).

You have undoubtedly heard Edwin Markham's "Parable of the Builders" on this subject. A certain rich man wanted to do good with his wealth, so he walked over his estate to see who was in need. He came to a little house down in a hollow where a carpenter lived with his very large family. A short while later, he sent for that carpenter and had him look over the plans of a very beautiful house. "I want you to build a house just like this over on that sunny hill." He instructed him to construct the house out of the finest materials, for he wanted it to be excellent. He then went away on a long journey and wouldn't return until the house was finished.

The carpenter seized his opportunity to pocket some profit for himself. He bought poor materials but charged the owner the price of the best. He skimped on the quality of his work, yet charged a high wage for it. The house looked adequate, but the carpenter knew what a flimsy piece of construction it was.

When the owner returned, he complimented his worker on the fine looking house, then handed him the key to it. All along, he had intended it for the carpenter and his large family. The builder was heartbroken as he walked away muttering, "Oh, if only I had known that I was building the house for myself!"

The consistent testimony of the Bible is that it is only through our giving that we receive, only in taking care of the needs of others that our own most important needs are met, only in serving God with generosity that we can expect the full generosity of God to be showered on us. Through our giving, we are in a very real sense "building the house" for ourselves.

... and Enrichingly

"You will be made rich in every way so that you can be generous on every occasion, and through us your generosity will result in thanksgiving to God" (2 Corinthians 9:11).

It could not be plainer, could it? If we sow generously, we *will* also reap generously. If we take control of our possessions without allowing them to possess us, God will make us all the richer so that we can be all the more generous.

There's a tombstone somewhere in an English village cemetery that bears this chilling epitaph:

Here lies a miser who lived for himself,
And cared for nothing but gathering pelf,
Now where he is or how he fares,
Nobody knows and nobody cares.

Contrast the miser's fate with that of a little widow who lived on a farm outside of Asheville, North Carolina. Back in 1919, her Baptist denomination announced a campaign to raise $75,000,000. This widow, who used the proceeds from her rocky farm to support her widowed daughter and three grandchildren, wanted to help her church, but she had very little to give.

On the morning she was to leave for Asheville to give her meager offering, her old workhorse had such a sore shoulder she didn't have the heart to harness it. So she walked eleven miles to town through a downpour of rain to make her contribution.

53

When she arrived, the church treasurer refused to take her money. The treasurer realized that her thirty-cent offering was all the money the widow had. She insisted though, telling the treasurer that she had prayed it through.

He was so moved by her generosity, and so ashamed of his own selfishness, that he quadrupled his own pledge. Then the next Wednesday, he told the story at the church prayer meeting. The word soon became known to the whole congregation, and then throughout Baptist churches around the world. A newpaper reporter was sent to North Carolina to investigate, and then published his findings. It was true.

She had so little, yet the Lord made her rich so that her generosity resulted in "thanksgiving to God." Her treasure was in Heaven; the impact of her value system was felt all around this earth.

Whom do you consider to be the victorious person, the rich young ruler, the miser who gathered his pelf, or the humble North Carolina widow? Who was freer? Who was happier? Who had the brightest future?

"You will be made rich," too, if you will let God give you victory over your possessions. Then "you can be generous on every occasion" and be the reason why others offer "thanksgiving to God."

In the end, only the generous win.

----

[1]Quoted in *Time* , January 23, 1984, p. 44.

[2]G. Curtis Jones, *What Are You Worth?* (St. Louis: Bethany Press, 1954), p. 20.

6
What to Do When You've Blown It
Matthew 26:31-35, 69-75

This book is about victory in Jesus. But some of its readers feel anything but victorious. I may be talking about you. You may have tried and failed. You feel your life is in shambles and you don't know how to put it back together again. You know you've blown it, but you don't know how to undo the damage.

What is even worse than your failure is your terrible, haunting fear of failing again.

I hope you will pay close attention in this chapter, because it's written especially for you. I must tell you at the outset that I'm going to be saying a good word about failing, and I am going to insist that you accept the difference between failing at something and being a failure. Far, far worse than failing is the fear of failure. And worse than fearing failure is believing that because you have failed, you are therefore a failure. That's a deadly untruth.

The problem with failing to achieve some objective is not in missing the goal but in mishandling ourselves when we fall short.

What Happens When We've Blown It?

We Become Defensive

We can't take criticism. We can't stand the thought that somebody might think us wrong in even the most insignificant issues. People can't get through to us. We won't allow them to make any suggestions that we think reflect critically on us. We won't allow them to hint at any imperfection in us, but not because we think we are perfect. We don't. It's because we are already persuaded we aren't that we shut our ears to anyone who agrees with us on this point. We can't stand any more proof of our inadequacy.

We Become Rigid

We won't change, because we are afraid that in any attempt to do so, we'll fail again.

We Lower Our Goals

When we were younger, we had high hopes for ourselves. We didn't realize them, so we've given up, settling for second best because we are convinced we can't achieve the best. Lower goals reduce the pressure.

We Make Excuses and Offer Rationalizations

We defend our less-than-desirable performance, finding circumstances or persons whom we can blame. We know we are at fault, but we will do and say anything to keep others from discovering this truth about ourselves.

Often We Become Sick

I wish there were a way to be statistically certain just how many of our illnesses are related to our sense of failure. Several doctors have told me they agree with studies indicating that from sixty to eighty percent of our illnesses are emotionally triggered. Those unhealthy emotions are often associated with failure.

Or We Give Up

We don't try anymore. We just put in our time waiting for the day that it's all over for us.

It isn't failure that does this to us. It's fear of failure. To learn how to handle failure, we need to study the apostle Peter, one of the most prominent "failures" in the Bible. What was so humiliating for Peter was that he had been so sure of himself. "All the rest of the fellows may let you down, Lord, but I won't. I'm one guy you can count on. Don't worry about me, Lord."

He is not only sure of himself, but he's now publicly committed. His fellow disciples have heard him boast. He has made them look bad in order to build up himself. You can bet they have taken note of it.

Don't misunderstand me here. Some people protect themselves from possible failure by never openly committing themselves to any goal. That way they never have to explain why they didn't achieve it. That may seem a safe course, but it's a deadend. It guarantees failure. If you want to accomplish something in life, announce your intentions to one or two other people. That invites them to hold you accountable. You don't have to be as boastful as Peter, but tell somebody what you intend to do. The very telling will strengthen your determination.

Peter believed in himself. He had no doubt that he would be true to Jesus, no matter what. He was fully prepared to succeed. I'm convinced he could have resisted a battalion of armed soldiers, but he was totally unprepared to resist a couple of girls.

I know how this works. As a minister, I have often prepared to do righteous battle for a cause. I've never been afraid of a board of elders nor of a congregation nor of city hall. But in every church, there has been the proverbial "little old lady." She'll win every time.

Peter was probably exhausted. The trauma of watching as his Lord was arrested and dragged away by armed ruffians, his own attempt to save his Lord with a sword, the confusion of shouts and shoves and insults, and his utter helplessness to stop the rush of events took their toll on Peter. You can understand, can't you? It's easy to be logical and reasonable when you are rested. It's at the end of the day, when you've been drained by the tensions of the job, that you make a fool of yourself and betray your best intentions.

Then, like Peter, you immediately regret it. And, like Peter, you feel like a complete failure.

What, then, should you do? Let me make some suggestions.

What You Can Do to Gain Victory

Admit You've Blown It

You aren't the first, you know. The difference between achievers and non-achievers is not that some fail and others succeed, or that some sin and others don't. The Bible states it clearly: "All have sinned and fall short of the glory of God" (Romans 3:23). The difference, then, is not in failing or not failing, but in what you do after you've blown it.

When you've sinned or failed, for Heaven's sake—for your sake—admit it. Start here.

As soon as Peter realized what he had done, he went off by himself and wept bitterly. We know the rest of the story as well. This man Peter, who let Jesus down in the moment when his Lord most needed his loyalty, became the very man God chose to preach the sermon on the Day of Pentecost when the church was born. It was this man who rose to preeminence among the apostles. Obviously, God wasn't finished with him yet! He failed, but that did not make him a failure.

Let me repeat myself. Whatever you do, don't equate failing at something with being a failure. That's not fair—not to you and not to God. When you do, you don't give God a second chance with you. You're denying Him the opportunity to do what He does best, giving rebirth, offering new life.

He can't do much with us, though, if we deny that we need the help. This kind of denial is lying, of course, and God can't reform us until we become honest with Him. Learn to say, "I was wrong."

Not long ago, Arizonans received a painful lesson in honesty. The publisher of our most powerful newspapers was found out. For thirty years he had been parading as a war hero, wearing his uniform, brandishing his medals, dropping names, advertising his rank. Then the attorney general, smarting because Duke Tully's newspapers had been a thorn in his side, got his sweet revenge. He published the truth: Tully had been lying about his war experiences and military career all those years. Overnight, Tully was in disgrace, his career ruined and his power vanquished.

How could this have happened to a man of his eminence? It was all very easy. Thirty years ago, he told one lie. Then he had to tell another to cover the first. From then on, he lived in fear that the first wrong would be discovered, so he told yet more lies. Probably in time, even he couldn't always tell the difference between his stories and the facts. (I resist the temptation to point out here that this disease sometimes afflicts journalists.) And it all began because sometime in the beginning, he didn't say, "I was wrong."

Who can say, "I'm always honest"? I remain convinced that our nation could have been spared the agonies of Watergate, and President Nixon would have completed his full term in office, if only he had said, "I've blown it."

How much freedom there is in admitting our sins or mistakes! How much peace comes from humbly saying, "I was wrong." So admit it.

Accept God's Forgiveness

A certain businessman acted dishonestly in one of his deals. He was discovered and exposed to public scandal. He disgraced himself and his family, especially his children, who had to suffer the taunts of their schoolmates. They loved their father, though, and they stuck by him. They forgave him.

He gratefully accepted their forgiveness, but there was one more thing he knew he had to do. He understood that dishonesty is not only a sin against people, but it is also a sin against the God of truth. He had to ask God's forgiveness as well. He had sinned

58

against God in failing to fulfill his responsibilities to his children, and in violating the trust of his wife, and in cheating his business partners. Like ours, his relationship with God was so intertwined with his relationship with other people that to act unjustly in the one was a sin in the other. He had to ask God's forgiveness.

When we ask, we can do so with confidence because of His promise: "If we claim to be without sin, we deceive ourselves and the truth is not in us. If we confess our sins, he is faithful and just and will forgive us our sins and purify us from all unrighteousness" (1 John 1:8, 9). All God asks is that we give Him a chance. He wants to purify us, to forgive us, to give us a new start.

In my teaching career, I used to lead my students through some of the ancient Greek and Roman dramas. It was not unusual for a playwright to tangle his plot up so tightly that there was no way out for the protagonists. No way, that is, except one. The *deus ex machina* (literally, the "god out of the machine") appeared in the final act to untangle and by divine fiat make things right. Only a god could do that. The Greek dramatists could effectively use this device because they and their audiences agreed that we sometimes so complicate our own life's plot that there is no way out except for help from above.

The human race hasn't improved any since the days of ancient Rome and Greece, so you don't need to be ashamed to admit that you were wrong. Accept the help and forgiveness that God offers.

Learn From It

If you are like me, you haven't learned much from your successes. I seem to learn everything the hard way, by failing first. Marcel Proust wrote that "illness is the most heeded of doctors: to goodness and wisdom we only make promises; we obey pain." It only takes a toothache to make us believe Proust's statement, doesn't it? Pain in the soul does as much to us as an ache in a bicuspid. Pain in the heart we pay attention to, the pain that comes through guilt, through embarrassment, through failing. We do learn from the pain of failure.

One of my favorite Vince Lombardi stories comes from Zig Ziglar. He says that during a pretty sorry practice session for the Green Bay Packers, Coach Lombardi vented his spleen on one big guard. He called him a lousy football player who wasn't blocking or tackling or putting out. He got so worked up he sent the guard to the showers.

59

Forty-five minutes later, when practice was over, Lombardi walked into the shower room and saw the big guard still sitting in uniform in front of his locker, quietly sobbing. The coach did an about face. He put his arm around the guard's shoulder. "Son," he told him, "I told you the truth. You are a lousy football player. You're not blocking, you're not tackling, you're not putting out. However, in all fairness to you, I should have finished the story. Inside of you, son, there is a great football player and I'm going to stick by your side until the great football player inside of you has a chance to come out and assert himself."[1]

Lombardi stuck to his word. Jerry Kramer, the guard, later gained fame as one of football's greatest, acknowledged as the all-time guard in professional football's first fifty years. He learned from his mistakes.

Peter was having a bad day. The man whom Jesus affectionately nicknamed "Rocky" turned jellyfish when his Lord needed him most. But Jesus stood by him and, in time, he became the leader of the apostles. He earned his nickname.

You are well acquainted with another man who let Jesus down. Interestingly enough, Judas didn't fail. He succeeded in doing precisely what he meant to do, and he earned some extra cash to boot. When he realized what he had accomplished, however, he was so overcome by his perfidy that he committed suicide. He didn't learn from his error; instead, he cut off any chance of his ever profiting from his mistake.

If Judas hadn't killed himself, I am convinced that the Lord would have rescued and remade him, doing for him what He did for Peter. It was Judas who cut off the Lord's forgiveness, not Jesus.

Refuse to Dwell on It or Make a Crutch of It

What I am about to say may not apply directly to you, but I know it is true of many of the readers of these pages. Some of you grew up in abject poverty; some were physically or sexually abused; some were terrified of angry, unreliable parents; many experienced the traumas of divorce. Others suffered in public school, others in bad neighborhoods, still others because of irrational prejudice against you. You may have gone hungry. You may have been neglected.

If you are among these, then I have a question for you. What are you going to do about your past? May I offer a word of advice?

Forget it. Don't make a crutch out of it, and don't let your past dictate your present behavior. You are an adult now. It's time to put away childish things. It's time to declare your independence of your childhood. It should no longer dominate you. Neither should you explain away your present failings by claiming to be unable to help yourself because of your past. "When I became a man, I put away childish things . . ." (1 Corinthians 13:22, KJV).

Recall the experiences of Joseph. From the beginning, his life seemed destined for failure. His problem was that he was the spoiled son of a doting father. It's as damaging to a child to spoil him as to beat him. His privileged position fostered an extreme case of sibling rivalry; his jealous older brothers hated him. They sold him into slavery.

He eventually was bought by the captain of Pharaoh's guard, who recognized Joseph's extraordinary abilities and in time placed him in charge of his household. When his prudery displeased Potiphar's wife, however, Joseph landed in the dungeon. The former slave was now a convict. I don't need to detail his suffering, nor the circumstances that led to his eventual rise in Pharaoh's administration to the position of Prime Minister in charge of administering Egypt's agricultural industry in preparation for and during the famine.

When famine hit his homeland, Joseph's father dispatched his remaining sons to Egypt to buy food. The person to whom they had to make their appeal was their brother. When Joseph saw them, he recognized immediately who they were. This was his moment for sweet revenge. He did not take vengeance, however. After a while, he identified himself to them. His words are unforgettable: "I am your brother Joseph, the one you sold into Egypt!" They must have prepared for the worst when they heard this. But Joseph fooled them. "And now, do not be distressed and do not be angry with yourselves for selling me here, because it was to save lives that God sent me ahead of you" (Genesis 45:4, 5). Seeing the hand of God in everything that had happened to him up to that point, Joseph accepted the bad as preparation for the service he could now render to God, to Egypt, and to his own family. From apparent disgrace and failure, he had risen to triumph.

What are you doing about the tragedy in your past? I hope you understand that it contributed to the making of the person you are today. It can, if you let it, help fashion the even better person you will be tomorrow. Turn that liability into an asset.

Build on It

There isn't a dark blotch in your past that you can't use to brighten somebody else's day. Let me tell you about a minister who learned this lesson. He was already in his fifties when he tried to break into book publishing. He sent his manuscript to several publishers. They sent him rejection slips. Finally, he had had enough. He threw his manuscript into his wastebasket and told his wife, "We've wasted enough time on it. I forbid you to take it from the wastebasket."

She wanted to try another publisher, but she didn't want to disobey her husband. She knew what to do. The publisher must have been quite surprised to see a dignified lady come into his office carrying a wastebasket. He was intrigued enough to rescue the manuscript from the container. He liked it, so Dr. Norman Vincent Peale's famous *The Power of Positive Thinking* went to press. It has since sold millions of copies.

We know Dr. Peale as one of America's most famous and successful writers and preachers, but one day, he felt like a failure. Thanks to his wife, he wasn't allowed to quit, and he has since built on that experience. You know about his books and his *Guidepost* magazine and his radio and television programs.

What about you? How are you now building on what you learned from those times when you thought you had blown it?

Can you join me in this prayer?

"Father, I'm sorry I have sinned against You, or have used bad judgment, or, quite simply, have just blown it.

"Thank You for promising to forgive me if I confess my sin. I'm confessing. I'm sorry.

"I accept the forgiveness You offer in Christ Jesus.

"I confess my faith as well as my sins. I give You my heart, my soul, my mind, my whole being. I want to be set free from my past.

"Please Father, reach Your hand to my hand and take from me my excuses, my rationalizations, my crutches, and my fear of failure. Help me to learn from my mistakes and to make a new beginning.

"Thank You, Lord. In Jesus' name, amen."

---

[1]Zig Ziglar, *See You at the Top* (Gretna, La.: Pelican Publishing Company, 1975), p. 112.

7

I Don't Doubt It
2 Timothy 1:3-12; Acts 9:1-19

The young man in my study was obviously distraught. A Christian for less than a year, he had embraced his new faith with enthusiasm and total acceptance of what he thought were Christian absolutes. Then he had enrolled in our nearby state university, where in several of his classes, his professors seemed determined to undermine everything he thought he believed. With unexpected suddenness, his new faith seemed about to collapse under the weight of intellectual doubts.

At first, he hesitated to confess them to me. He was fearful of rejection, yet he had to be honest. He had been led to believe, he told me, that "if you doubt, you're not a Christian."

Fortunately, we were meeting in my study, surrounded on every wall by books from ceiling to floor. To encourage him, I simply pointed to them and said, "Just look around you. Do you think that a man who surrounds himself with this much literature on the subject has never had any doubts about his faith?"

I was reminded of an old story of a college student's visit to Phillips Brooks, the famous preacher. "Dr. Brooks," he told him, "I would like to talk over some of my doubts; but I don't want to disturb your faith." The good man threw back his head and laughed. He had worked his way through to a solid faith only by honestly confronting the many questions that his academic career had thrown at him. Nothing this student could say would frighten him now.

You can't help admiring the honesty of these young men, can you? There is hope in such integrity. God doesn't want us to pretend a faith that isn't true.

Some time ago, I asked a mature Christian woman how she has handled her doubts through the years. (I didn't ask her whether she had any; I just assumed so. It's a pretty nigh universal experience.) She told me, "I don't panic. I put the doubt on hold while I investigate the issue. In time I work my way through it."

She didn't realize how close her approach was to that of the sixteenth-century man of letters, Francis Bacon. In *De Augmentis,* he wrote, "If we begin with certainties, we will end in doubt. But if we begin with doubts and bear them patiently, we may end in certainty."

Can you imagine the pain that Saul of Tarsus must have felt when the Lord confronted him on the road to Damascus (see Acts 9:1-19). He was on the way to Damascus in his fanatical pursuit of Christians, hoping to stamp out this heresy before it could do any more damage. Then came brilliant light and the probing voice of the Lord, and then the blindness. A helpless, humbled Saul had to receive the ministrations of Ananias, one of those hated Christians.

What was he to think, this Pharisee of the Pharisees, this rising young leader of the Jews, when the Lord told him that his career had been in vain, that he had, in fact, been persecuting the Lord he thought he had been serving? Don't you think he had some doubts—about himself, about his beliefs, about his former teachers, about his whole society? Of course he did. Thank God he did, because they opened his mind to find the truth.

There was a critical moment in Jesus' ministry, when He had been teaching some hard, demanding truths about discipleship. Many of His followers heard Him, understood Him, and therefore left Him. He turned to His Twelve and asked, "You do not want to leave too, do you?"

Simon Peter answered for all of them: "Lord, to whom shall we go? You have the words of eternal life. We believe and know that you are the Holy One of God" (John 6:67-69). They weren't always so certain, but they had observed His ministry, had studied the Scriptures with Him, and had concluded that Jesus was who He claimed to be. It isn't that they wouldn't doubt again—they would at His trial, for example—but then when God provided the proof through the resurrection, their faith was justified.

Doubt. It's so integral a part of faith that you cannot really conceive of one without the other.

The Bible affords us a good study of the subject in Paul's letter to his younger apprentice Timothy (see 2 Timothy 1:3-12).

A Picture of Doubt: Is Timothy Struggling With It?

Paul's language in 2 Timothy 1 hints that Timothy is, indeed, struggling with doubt. He refers to "a spirit of timidity" and encourages Timothy not to "be ashamed to testify about our Lord" nor, for that matter, to be embarrassed that his mentor is a prisoner. Timidity is often born of uncertainty. When you are dead certain you are right, you don't hesitate. And, of course, if you are right, you aren't ashamed, either. Perhaps Timothy has some doubts, either about himself or God or the future of the church, which has grown so unpopular in so many circles. It isn't easy to "testify about our Lord" when all the powers seem to be against you. There is Timothy's teacher, in prison. If he were truly speaking of God, would he now be locked up? Is this how God treats His spokesmen? Perhaps Timothy is even rethinking Jesus' place in God's scheme of things. He was, after all, a pretty unlikely Messiah—an apparent failure, dying like a criminal, the avowed enemy of the entire Jewish religious establishment.

Whatever Timothy has been thinking, Paul seems to realize he needs encouragement, like the young man in my study. I assured him that there is no need to be embarrassed about doubt. It is often a very good thing. There are some fairly strong reasons for doing it.

In the first place, we doubt because of the inconsistencies between the proclamation and the practices of the church. Listen to Paul's exalted language here: "Our Savior, Christ Jesus ... has destroyed death and has brought life and immortality to light through the gospel" (2 Timothy 1:10). What an enormous claim Paul is making. Yet when Timothy looked around, he saw tiny churches struggling for survival against the overwhelming power of Judaism and the Roman Empire. Had Jesus, in fact, destroyed death?

In later years, the church, no longer tiny but the ruling power of the world, gave thoughtful people everywhere ample reason to doubt the claims of Christianity. One has only to mention the "holy" crusades, the Spanish Inquisition, the superstitions, the dogmatism, the hypocrisy and ignorance of the clergy, the book-burnings and the witch burnings, the fear and conformity of the laity, and many other excesses of an institution that exchanged spiritual power for political, to conclude that something was dreadfully amiss in the church Jesus founded. What kind of a God has done this?

You can fairly answer, of course, that this is not so much what God has done to man as what man has done to man and to God in the name of God. Fortunately, I have spent some time in the company of atheists. They have helped me realize that Christians do not have the corner on dogmatism or its attending evils. In fact, the atheists are every bit as dogmatic and for less reason. They demand that we replace faith in God with faith in them, in their intelligence and their values. I so much appreciated one honest man who admitted that it takes a lot of faith to be an atheist. More, it seems to me, than to believe in the God of the Bible.

The embarrassing truth is that the church has made many misleading promises through the years. Robert Fife reports that his infantry division in 1944 was soon to be ordered overseas when a well-meaning preacher sent the chaplain a package of tracts to be distributed to his men. The tract promised, "If you truly believe in God, you won't be hit. God will not allow any evil to befall you."

Chaplain Fife wisely threw the tracts into the wastebasket. He knew that God's Word does not teach that only unbelievers are vulnerable to machine gun and artillery fire.

It's perfectly fair to entertain doubts about farfetched promises like this one that unthinking people blithely hand out in the name of the church.

We sometimes doubt because some questions are hard to answer. Very dear friends of ours lost a child to Sudden Infant Death Syndrome ("crib death"). Why? Others lost their teenage son when an automobile struck him as he was riding his bicycle home from school. Why? A special couple in our church have had to rebuild their lives after their teenaged son and daughter were killed as they were driving home from church. Why? Twentieth-century citizens have been subjected to the worst imaginable horrors of war, and God-fearing men and women and children have been slaughtered. Why? It has long been observed that the wicked prosper and the righteous go without. Again, why?

Should we tell inquiring young minds that these questions ought not to disturb them? Not at all. A faith that does not wrestle with these honest questions is not adequate to sustain twentieth-century believers.

Sometimes we doubt because we want to grow. Another young Christian college student came to see me recently. He had been thinking through some of these tough questions. A well-meaning friend had told him that Christians are merely to trust and never to ask questions or try to understand the mind of God. How unfortunate. The young man was about to turn his back on a Christianity that would forbid him to think. I assured him that when he became a Christian, he didn't give up his mind. He is, in fact, to love the Lord with all his heart and soul and *mind*.

It was the brilliant Russian writer Dostoevsky who confessed, "My hosannas have been forged in the crucible of doubt." The theologian Paul Tillich admitted, "Sometimes I think my mission is to bring faith to the faithless and doubt to the faithful."

Whether Tillich is right or not is debatable, but he at least recognizes that the church is in the education business. We are teaching Christ. Unfortunately, many Christians believe it to be their responsibility to attend worship in order to hear what they already are convinced of, and they don't readily tolerate any deviation from their set convictions. If people want to grow, however, they must be willing to have their convictions challenged from time to time. Genuine faith welcomes the challenge.

Sometimes we doubt because we want our faith to be true. Just as an untried virtue is no virtue at all, so an untested faith is not really faith. So we raise questions. This only makes sense, for we are investing a lifetime in our faith. We do not want to learn on the Judgment Day that we were wrong all along. We want it to be true.

At other times, we doubt because we fear that our faith is true. The frightening thing about religious faith is that it has consequences. A true believer acts out his belief. He is obedient to it. "Why is it so hard to believe?" the great Pascal asks. "Because it is so hard to obey," he answers. It's easier to suspend belief, to proclaim our doubts, than to commit ourselves to a course of action that demands obedience to a Master.

As a student, Horace Bushnell thought he was an atheist. One day, a voice seemed to say to him, "If you do not believe in God, what do you believe?"

"I believe there is a difference between right and wrong," he answered. This seemed to be the best he could do.

"Are you living up to the highest you believe?" the voice then demanded to know.

"No, but I will." Right then, Bushnell dedicated his life to his highest belief. That minimal obedience led him in time to a greater faith. Charles Allen, who tells this story in *God's Psychiatry,* adds that when Bushnell "began conforming his life to his beliefs, instead of making his beliefs fit his life, he was led to a realization of God."[1]

The Spirit of Faith

If we are right in thinking Paul's letter to Timothy suggests that the young man may have been entertaining some doubts, then we are most certainly correct in finding in this passage a helpful description of the spirit of faith.

A believer has a spirit of sincerity. He exhibits "sincere faith." He is what he seems to be.

He has a spirit of power. Instead of timidity, he displays courage and strength. His is not an "on the one hand, on the other" faith. God gives him the strength to decide and then to be steadfast in pursuing the course he has chosen.

He has a spirit of love. The anonymous author of *The Cloud of Unknowing* has asserted, "By love God may be gotten and holden, but by thought or understanding, never." He goes too far, but in the right direction. God is love, and His children are loving as well. George MacDonald insists that "nothing helps many, perhaps all, to believe in God so much as the active practical love of the neighbor." How often in counseling doubting young Christians I have encouraged them to act as if they believe. The act is the father of the thought.

He has a spirit of self-discipline. Unpopular words, these, in this self-indulgent era, but necessary. I have long observed that doubt—self-doubt, doubt about God, doubt about the meaning of life—always follows the undisciplined person wherever he goes.

He has a willingness to suffer for the gospel. In verses eight and twelve, Paul invites Timothy to suffer with him, because the good news of new life in Jesus is worth suffering for.

The Source of Faith That Conquers

That last sentence is what makes all the difference to Paul: "New life in Jesus is worth suffering for." Here is the source of his faith: it's in a person, and the person is Jesus: "I am not ashamed, because I know *whom* I have believed, and am convinced that *he* is able to guard what I have entrusted to him for that day" (2 Timothy 1:12). His life, the young churches he has established, his reputation, his daily needs, his destiny—everything is in the Lord's hands.

He hasn't always felt this way, obviously. Return for a moment to that dramatic encounter on the road to Damascus. He was bound for that city to bind up Christians, dead certain that he was doing precisely what God wanted him to do. And he was dead wrong. What a jumble of doubts and questions must have jammed his mind that day. He would never be the same afterward. He was in for a transformation of purpose and practice that nothing short of a personal encounter with the living Lord could have effected.

But then, that's what always lifts us above our doubts, isn't it? Somewhere Rudolf Bultmann has written, "The transfer of faith from the dimension of a personal encounter into the dimension of factual instruction is the great tragedy of Christianity." It had been Paul's personal tragedy as well. He was learned in the Hebrew Scriptures. He was able to debate fine points of the law with the best of his contemporaries. He had been taught by experts; he himself became an expert in "the dimension of factual instruction." But he hadn't yet met the living Lord.

Nor have many of our contemporaries. They have studied the Bible, read the commentaries, attended the sermons, and missed the relationship. Christian faith is personal. It cannot be reduced to a mere adherence to a creed nor a compliance with ritual. It is quite personal, a spiritual binding of our spirits with the Spirit of God.

Andrae Crouch has captured something of this faith above doubt in his popular "Through It All":

I've had many tears and sorrows;
I've had questions for tomorrow;
There've been times I didn't know right from wrong;
But in ev'ry situation God gave blessed consolation
That my trials come to only make me strong.

I've been to lots of places,
And I've seen a lot of faces;
There've been times I felt so all alone;
But in my lonely hours, yes, those precious lonely hours,
Jesus let me know that I was His Own.

I thank God for the mountains,
And I thank Him for the valleys;
I thank Him for the storms He brought me through;
For if I'd never had a problem,
I wouldn't know that He could solve them,
I'd never know what faith in God could do.

Through it all,
Through it all
Oh, I've learned to trust in Jesus,
I've learned to trust in God.
Through it all,
Through it all
Oh I've learned to depend upon His Word.[2]

Doesn't this song sound like Paul's total trust in the One in whom he has believed?

During the bleak days of the London Blitz, when Hitler's Nazi pilots were pummelling the city night after night, a father grabbed his son's hand and ran from a building that had been struck by a bomb. He spotted a large shell hole in the front yard, and quickly jumped into it for shelter. He turned around and lifted up his arms for his son to jump into.

The little boy was too frightened to jump, even though he wanted to do what his father was asking. "I can't see you," he yelled.

He was looking down into the black hole. The father, however, could see him, for the boy was silhouetted against the sky that the burning buildings had turned into a reddish glow. "But I can see you," he told his son. "Jump."

He trusted his father and was soon safe in his arms.

"I know whom I have believed . . . he is able."

---

[1]Charles Allen, *God's Psychiatry* (Old Tappan, NJ: Fleming H. Revell Co., 1953), p. 38.

[2]Andrae Crouch, "Through It All." © Copyright 1971 by Manna Music, Inc., 2111 Kenmere Ave., Burbank, CA 91504. International copyright secured. Used by permission.

8

Why Doesn't Everybody Like Me?

Matthew 7:1-5; John 15:18-25; Acts 9:20-31

From Jewish folklore comes this poignant story of unfair rejection. A young man is riding on the train to Lublin, Poland. Trying to make small talk with an older merchant, he opens with a surefire conversation starter. "Can you tell me the time?"

The merchant tells him, in direct terms, where he can go.

"What?" the astonished young man asks. "I ask you a simple question and you answer with rudeness. Why, what's the matter with you?"

The merchant sighs wearily, tells him to sit down, and begins his explanation. "All right, I'll tell you what's the matter. You ask me a question. I have to give you an answer, no? That starts a conversation. We talk about the weather, politics, business, and so on. One thing leads to another. It turns out you're a Jew. I'm a Jew. I live in Lublin, you're a stranger there. Out of hospitality, I must ask you to my home for dinner. You meet my daughter. She's a beautiful girl; you're a handsome young man. You date a few times. You fall in love. Finally, you come to ask for my daughter's hand in marriage. So why go to all that trouble? Let me tell you right now, young man, I won't let my daughter marry anyone who doesn't even own a watch!"

Rejection. Who hasn't felt it? How can I sing with my fellow Christians, "It is well with my soul," when I'm suffering rejection, sometimes even from my brothers in the faith? Yet my condition isn't exceptional, is it? Who hasn't asked, "Why don't they like me?" Let's explore some answers.

It May Be That You Are in the Wrong

I stopped briefly to pick up something at a local shopping center. When I returned to my car, I found a small yellow card stuck beneath the windshield wiper. On it was this professionally printed message:

THANKS FOR TAKING
TWO PARKING SPACES
I Had To Park Two Blocks Away
You Stupid Inconsiderate Moron

I could feel my face turning red, whether from embarrassment or indignation I wasn't sure. I like to pride myself on my considerate driving practices. So I checked to find out that, sure enough, I was right on the line. It was possible for a car to squeeze into the space beside me, but with difficulty. I was guilty as charged.

Let's face it, some of the criticism we receive we deserve. This is the hardest kind to take. We put up our defenses. We blame our accuser, indignantly pointing out that he has no right to point out our flaws, since he is so full of them himself. We can even hurl a Scripture at him: "You, therefore, have no excuse, you who pass judgment on someone else, for at whatever point you judge the other, you are condemning yourself, because you who pass judgment do the same things" (Romans 2:1). This is the principle of psychological projection, about which we'll have more to say in a moment. For right now, though, the fact remains, we may be wrong.

It May Be That You Aren't Likeable

Are you too loud, too boastful, too sullen, too moody? Are you hypocritical, pretending a piety you don't practice? Or do you practice a piety that demeans other less righteous ones? Does your language—either pious or profane or too plain—make other people uncomfortable? Are you always honest? Always loving? Always kind? Do you have a critical spirit, quick to describe another's shortcomings and just as quick to forgive your own? You'll recognize Jesus' words on the subject:

> Do not judge, or you too will be judged. For in the same way you judge others, you will be judged, and with the measure you use, it will be measured to you.
>
> Why do you look at the speck of sawdust in your brother's eye and pay no attention to the plank in your own eye? How can you say to your brother, "Let me take the speck out of your eye," when all the time there is a plank in your own eye? You hypocrite, first take the plank out of your own eye, and then you will see clearly to remove the speck from your brother's eye (Matthew 7:1-5).

72

The Christian's first concern, as Jesus explains, is to help your neighbor ("to remove the speck from your brother's eye"). That's pretty difficult to do when you can't see clearly. This impediment moves Paul to refer to some critical Christians as the *weaker* brothers in Romans 14 and 1 Corinthians 8. Undoubtedly, nothing alienates us from other people as quickly as our own judgmental attitude. Nobody willingly hangs around his personal put-downer.

It May Be Because You're Not One of Them

Jesus has warned His disciples not to expect to be appreciated:

If the world hates you, keep in mind that it hated me first. If you belonged to the world, it would love you as its own. As it is, *you do not belong to the world,* but I have chosen you out of the world. *That is why the world hates you.* Remember the words I spoke to you: "No servant is greater than his master." If they persecuted me, they will persecute you also. If they obeyed my teaching, they will obey yours also. They will treat you this way because of my name, for they do not know the One who sent me (John 15:18-21).

Jesus is speaking specifically of His and His disciples' persecutors, but His warning can be applied in much broader terms. I'm thinking of terrorism, for example, which has held the world in its frightful grip for years now. Politicians are scrambling to find peaceful ways to fight it while military leaders propose their simpler but deadlier solutions. It's not going to go away, though, because it thrives on its own hatred. The terrorist message is clear: "I hate you because you're not like me." At the root of anti-Americanism, anti-Semitism, racism, ageism, sexism, and political, religious, and class wars of every distinction is this unreasonable, all-consuming hatred. Thus we categorize and divide and subdivide humanity into easily identifiable pigeonholes so that we can heap scorn and contempt on all who aren't quite like us. As long as people hate each other for no other reason than "you're not like me," violence will terrorize this race.

When Joy and I were visiting in India, we spent a day at the beach in the South. Our hostess for the day proved an exceptional tour guide, and in that one day we learned a great deal about Indian culture. While we were enjoying a snack in a restaurant, at another table there was a group of four or five men. Our hostess explained that they were from North India. We couldn't discern any distinguishing characteristics, so we asked her how she could tell. "Oh," she said, "that's easy. North Indians are lighter skinned than South Indians." We studied them more closely, then looked at her, then back at them. We still couldn't tell the difference. She, a South Indian, had a much fairer complexion than they did, yet it was obvious to her that they were somehow "lighter."

Her culture had taught her to make these fine distinctions. It had instructed her on the importance of knowing that "they" are not like "us." As objective outsiders, Joy and I couldn't discriminate. Yet back home in America, we could have easily categorized people in ways that would have thoroughly confused our Indian hostess. Our culture had taught us how. It had even suggested which ones we should hate because they are different. This devilish ability to discriminate makes us all prime candidates for terrorist activity, as either recipients or participants.

You may know these immortal lines:

Believe as I believe—no more, no less;
That I am right (and no one else) confess.
Feel as I feel, think only as I think;
Eat what I eat, and drink what I drink.
Look as I look, do always as I do;
And then—and only then—I'll fellowship with you.

This attitude governs in all things great and small. Charles Swindoll (from whom I borrowed the above lines) tells of two congregations of different denominations that were located only a few blocks from each other in a small community. It was obvious that they would be better off if they would merge into one stronger church. They set things in motion to effect the merger, but they had to call it off. The immovable object proved to be the Lord's Prayer. One group believed the correct wording was "forgive us our trespasses" and the other "forgive us our debts." Since neither group could forgive the other's trespasses (or debts) in this difference of opinion, the deal was off. "They aren't like us" won again.[1]

In such little absurdities as this church dispute and in the great atrocities like international terrorism, the cause is the same. To insist that you have to be like me is to assume that I am the measure of perfection. You must be perfect as I am perfect. I will kill, if necessary, to protect "my kind" from attack or mutation. This is seen with frightening clarity in the death of one disfigured baby.

It happened in July, 1983. Dr. Daniel McKay, a thirty-five-year-old veterinarian in the Chicago suburb of Harvey, made the national news. Enjoying a reputation of excellence in his care of animals and gentle compassion as the father of his six-year-old daughter, Dr. McKay did not seem to be the kind of person who would stand accused of the crime the newspapers reported.

In the delivery room of Ingalls Memorial Hospital, Dr. McKay reportedly picked up and briefly held his newborn son, John Francis, born with a cleft palate and clenched hands. Then he dashed the baby against the floor, not once but twice. John Francis lived only twenty-nine minutes after his birth. Apparently, Dr. McKay couldn't accept a son with any kind of deformity. His son wasn't like him. He was imperfect.

When I read the newspaper account of this father's murder of his own son, I shuddered because more than once in my ministry, a distraught father has threatened murder. "I'll kill him," he has said. "I know it's wrong, but I'll kill him." The son had disgraced the father through crime or deviant sexual behavior or disobedience. Imperfect.

What do you do with people who look or act different? What should people do with you when *you're* the different one? As a disciple of Jesus, you have deliberately chosen a life-style that is not in conformity with the values of this world. What should the world do with you?

Yes, Jesus said to His disciples, they will hate you because you are not like them. "You are not of this world." You do not meet their standards. Interesting, isn't it? Christians are often criticized for seeming to look with reproach on non-Christians. Yet that criticism cuts both ways, doesn't it? Christians can't expect to be thought above reproach by the world. We have rejected the world's ways in accepting Christ; we are foolish if we expect the world to applaud.

It May Be Because of *Their* Guilt

If I had not come and spoken to them, they would not be guilty of sin. Now, however, they have no excuse for their sin. He who hates me hates my Father as well. If I had not done among them what no one else did, they would not be guilty of sin (John 15:22-24).

In Dostoevsky's masterpiece, *The Brothers Karamazov,* one of the characters longed to revenge himself on everyone for his own shortcomings. When he was asked why he hated a certain person so much, he answered, "I'll tell you. He has done me no harm. But I played him a dirty trick, and ever since then I have hated him." Have you ever been guilty of doing wrong against someone and then finding you couldn't stand to be around that person? It's in this sense that we can understand what happened at the cross. Jesus' enemies could find no fault with Him. The fault was in them. That's why they raged to kill Him.

I mentioned the principle of psychological projection earlier in this chapter. It simply states the obvious, that we most quickly condemn in others the fault of which we ourselves are guilty. Jesus is referring to it in His comments about the beam in your eye.

A literal illustration of this has been provided by Sir Percival Lowell, the famed astronomer who announced that there were canals on Mars. In 1877, he had heard that an Italian astronomer had seen straight lines crisscrossing the Martian surface. Intrigued, Sir Percival devoted the rest of his life to mapping the channels and canals he saw there. He believed they proved that there was intelligent life on Mars. His teachings were universally accepted. When twentieth-century space probes orbited Mars and landed on its surface, however, no canals were found. How could Lowell have been so certain—and so wrong?

We now know that Sir Percival suffered from a rare eye disease (named "Lowell's Syndrome" after the famed astronomer) that made him see the blood vessels in his own eyes. The "canals" he saw were the projections of his own veins.

As Jesus warned us not to criticize another for our own faults, Christians can take comfort in the knowledge that much of the criticism we receive is really a veiled confession of guilt on the part of our critics. They are seeing the canals in their own eyes.

Then—What's a Christian to do?

This is the real question, isn't it? Since it seems inevitable that we must suffer criticism, we want to know how a Christian is to meet it. Here are six suggestions that have helped me.

Listen

There might be some truth in what they are saying. You could learn from them.

When I was in college, one of my dormmates took it upon himself to let me know everything that was wrong with me. His charges stung, but I wouldn't give him the satisfaction of thinking he had got to me. Later, I asked a trusted friend about the criticism. He agreed with my critic. I was glad then that I hadn't remained too defensive to pay attention to this helpful advice. Instead, I began working to eliminate my offensive behavior. Sometimes your critics are right.

Laugh

If you don't take yourself too seriously, you can't be too seriously wounded by your critic's barbs. I recently received another copy of a letter that has been around for years. It still makes me laugh. It purports to be from a Reverend Elton Johns of the Rescue Mission in Canton, Ohio. It was addressed to me.

> My dear friend in the Lord:
> Perhaps you have heard of me in my nationwide campaign in the cause of temperance. Each year for the past fourteen years, I have made a tour of Florida, Georgia, Indiana, Iowa, Illinois, and Ohio. I have delivered a series of lectures on the evils of drinking. On this tour, I have been accompanied by my friend and assistant, Clyde Lindstrom. Clyde, a young man of good family and excellent background, is a pathetic example of a life ruined by excessive indulgence in whiskey and women.
> Clyde would appear with me at the lectures and sit on the platform, wheezing and staring at the audience through bleary, bloodshot eyes, sweating profusely and babbling incoherently, while I would point him out as an example of what overindulgence can do to a person.
> Last summer, unfortunately, Clyde died. A mutual friend has given me your name and I wonder if you would be available to take Clyde's place on my winter tour?

What fun I've had with this letter. It's absurd. It's ridiculous. And it's a surefire laugh at a party.

What are *you* going to do when people laugh at you? May I make a suggestion? Beat 'em to the draw. Laugh first. So you're not as tall as you'd like to be? Laugh about it. So your car is so old the dealer offers you money *not* to trade it in? Laugh about it. So your health isn't as dependable as it used to be? Laugh about it. So you weren't the first in your class? Laugh about it. I have a friend who has brightened many a conversation with his one-liner about his low I.Q. "I'm not doing so bad for a 78."

My predecessor in Indianapolis has built a career on Harlan County, Kentucky, jokes. He's one of the smartest hillbillies I've ever known, capitalizing to the hilt on his modest start in life.

So you think you're funny looking? Haven't you noticed that almost everybody is? I'm the only one in my family who isn't!

So you're afraid they'll find your flaws? Point them out before they get a chance to. If you're already laughing at yourself, somebody else's laughter can't hurt you.

Remember the Critic's Fate

A young musician's concert was poorly received by the critics. He was consoled by the famous Finnish composer Jean Sibelius, who patted him on the shoulder and said, "Remember, son, there is no city in the world where they have erected a statue to a critic." It's the critic's fate to be forgotten.

There are sportswriters and literary critics and drama critics. But they are all on the sidelines watching. They aren't in the play.

Be Thankful

After all, they think you are important or they wouldn't bother criticizing you. Politicians know this. It doesn't bother them so much to be openly opposed as to be quietly ignored. When Robert Schuller asked his friend, the late Congressman Clyde Doyle, how he could stand up against unfair treatment, he said,

> In politics we have the idea that even criticism helps us. The important thing to a politician is not, what are they saying about him, but are they talking about him? Even criticism is better than nothing. As long as people talk about us our names will be known. When the voters come to the ballot box the majority vote for a familiar name. Most of them still remember the name long after they have forgotten what was said about the man.[2]

I've had to give this advice to the congregation I serve in Arizona. There was a day when Central Christian Church was a cozy little group of people meeting in a cozy little building. The church could do whatever the members wanted and nobody noticed. Then the church began to take flight like a not altogether predictable and sometimes erratic but nonetheless regal butterfly. As the growth came, so did the criticism. "Look what they're doing over at that church." Now we can't do anything without attracting attention—and objection. God has called us to greater service, wider ministry, more public notoriety, and increased criticism.

You see, you can't escape it if you are doing what the Lord wants you to do. But you *can* reserve the right to choose what your critics are going to criticize you for.

The experience of Saul of Tarsus is a supreme example of this principle. In his pre-Christian days, Saul was chief of the young Christian church's persecutors. He enjoyed the praise of his fellow believers but, of course, was anathema to the Christians. Then came his dramatic conversion on the road to Damascus. He immediately began preaching "that Jesus is the Son of God." His former allies did not let many days elapse before they turned in wrath against him. They "conspired to kill him." His new friends helped him escape under cover of darkness (by lowering him in a basket through an opening in the city wall).

He repaired to Jerusalem to find safety among the large body of Christians there. They shut him out. Of course. How could they know that his conversion was for real? If it had not been for their highly respected Barnabas, who "took him and brought him to the apostles," Saul would have remained an outsider in Jerusalem (Acts 9:20-31).

When Saul turned his life over to Christ, he did not escape criticism. He merely changed critics. Then with the advance in his ministry as the apostle Paul, the noise of the critics grew louder. The more successful he became, the more intense was their criticism. When he later wrote in 1 Thessalonians 5:18, "Give thanks in all circumstances," he probably had even his rejection by his critics in mind.

Turn the Mud They're Slinging Into a Merit Badge

I picked up this little idea from the police. Back in the 1960s and 1970s, demonstrators frequently hurled verbal abuse at policemen trying to control unruly crowds. "PIGS!" they screamed. One enterprising policeman didn't take offense. "Of course, we're pigs," he said. "That stands for **P**atience, **I**ntegrity, and **G**uts."

That's what you do—turn their mud into a merit badge. This has been the Christian strategy throughout history. Clear back in the beginning, when people were hissing "Christians" as a term of contempt, disciples of Jesus accepted the term and made it one of honor. The Quakers did the same later, as did the Methodists and just about every other initially-despised Christian group.

Stay Close to the Source of Your Strength

Serve the Lord, and Him only. When Thomas Edison, a lifelong Republican, astonished his friends by jumping on Democrat Woodrow Wilson's presidential campaign bandwagon, he told them, "They say
Wilson has blundered. Well, I reckon he has, but I notice he always blunders *forward*." The critics of religion say that the church has blundered, and Christians are blundering. Well, they are right. But we do seem to be stumbling in the right direction, don't we? We are moving Christward. We have heard the Lord:

"If you belonged to the world, it would love you as its own. As it is, you do not belong to the world, but I have chosen you out of the world" (John 15:19).

We have heard Him, and we hear Him still!

---

[1]Charles Swindoll, *Growing Strong in the Seasons of Life* (Portland: Multnomah Press, 1983), p. 286.

[2]Robert Schuller, *Move Ahead with Possibility Thinking* (New York: Doubleday and Company, 1967), p. 92.

9

When You Feel All Alone
Acts 9:20-31

Malcolm Muggeridge has written, "The first thing I remember about the world—and I pray it may be the last—is that I was a stranger in it." Muggeridge calls this feeling, "the glory and the desolation of *homosapiens*."[1]

It hits everybody, this feeling of being a stranger, an alien. Alien—alienated. Lonely. Left behind. Rejected. Single adults sometimes think loneliness is the peculiar curse of their status, but it attacks married adults as well—and teenagers and children and old people and married parents and single parents.

Life in the city seems to take its toll as well. More than a century ago, when American cities were tiny compared with today's megalopolises, Henry David Thoreau described city life as "millions of people being lonely together." In modern America, where the average person moves about fourteen times in his life span, it's no wonder that so many of us nomads are lonely. Our values of personal independence, individualism, and competitiveness have ripped us apart. What's left of us feels hurt and rejected.

We turn for relief to a whole catalogue of surefire nostrums, hoping that workaholism or leisure or drink or drugs or sex or psychiatry or *something,* anything, will make us feel we belong.

We even "try religion." It's no secret—and no sin—that people turn to the church as much for social as for any other reason. They are seeking acceptance.

But what they sometimes find instead is rejection. There's precedent, because this is exactly what the apostle Paul first experienced as a new Christian. Read again Acts 9:20-31. What a disappointment was in store for the new convert, Saul of Tarsus. When he yielded his life to Christ, his former friends turned on him with a vengeance, conspiring to kill him. He should have been able to find shelter with his new Christian brothers and sisters. When he arrived in Jerusalem, however, he ran into doors slammed tight against him. If Barnabas hadn't had the courage to befriend him when no one else would, where could Paul have turned?

Rejection. Loneliness. "It is not good for the man to be alone," God observed of the solitary Adam (Genesis 3:18). It still isn't. It's painful, even more painful than being with people, which is why we dare to run the risks of social intercourse even when we know we almost certainly will get hurt.

What word of encouragement, then, can I give someone—maybe you—suffering from a sense of rejection and loneliness? Let me remind you of four facts of your life as a Christian which are easily forgotten when we're brooding in our solitude. I'll begin with the most obvious:

You Have the Lord

Did you study S. T. Coleridge's famous "Rime of the Ancient Mariner" when you were in high school? Coleridge describes a derelict whose deck is strewn with corpses. Only one old seaman survives. The poem is a picture of utter loneliness. The Mariner bemoans his fate in lines that Paul couldn't have thought of:

> Alone, alone, all all alone
> Alone on the wide wide Sea;
> And Christ would take no pity on
> my soul in agony.

> The many men so beautiful
> And they all dead did lie!
> And a million million slimy things
> Liv'd on—and so did I.

Paul was certain that, because of Christ, he was no longer to be compared with some "slimy" thing; he was equally convinced that it was through Christ's compassion on his "soul in agony" that Paul now enjoyed real life in Him. When you walk with the Lord, you have proof of His faithfulness to His promise, "Lo, I am with you *always.*"

A later Christian leader, F. W. Robertson of Brighton, England, described himself as a lonely man, "alone as my Master was," alienated from some who once loved him. He could accept their rejection, though, because "knowing that the Father is with me, I am not afraid to be alone." He admits that, "to a man not urgently

82

made, there is some sharpness in the thought" of his enforced solitude, but "a sublime feeling of a Presence comes about me at times which makes inward solitariness a trifle to talk about."[2] He was experiencing the truth in that wonderful hymn we sing,

O Love that wilt not let me go,
I rest my weary soul on Thee;
I give Thee back the life I owe,
That in Thine ocean depths its flow
May richer, fuller be.

It is a love that nothing—and nobody—can destroy. Much later in his ministry, a grateful apostle could write of it to the Romans:

For I am convinced that neither death nor life, neither angels nor demons, neither the present nor the future, nor any powers, neither height nor depth, nor anything else in all creation, will be able to separate us from the love of God that is in Christ Jesus our Lord (Romans 8:38, 39).

This is the tenacious love of a close friend who stands by you through everything, even when you are wrong. (As Mark Twain has said, "The proper office of a friend is to side with you when you are in the wrong. Nearly anybody will side with you when you are in the right!")

What a pleasure it was to run across the story on this subject of a young immigrant to America, Michael Pupin. When the immigration officer in New York asked the young man whether he had any friends in America, he answered that he did. The officer asked for their names. Pupin quickly told him that his friends were Benjamin Franklin, Abraham Lincoln, and Harriet Beecher Stowe. The official decided that with friends like these, the young man deserved to be admitted to America.

We seldom think of Pupin's friends as ours, do we? But they are. Unfortunately, we may be equally guilty of forgetting "what a friend we have in Jesus." Yet if we genuinely believe in Him, and if we trust that He is with us in His Spirit, we aren't really alone, are we? When you name your friends, start with Jesus. This isn't some kind of spiritual pep talk. It is merely a recognition of the fact that God, in Christ, came to us. His Spirit abides with us and we are not alone. Hang on to that fact.

You Have Your Ministry

This may not sound like much consolation at first, but after a little thought, I'm sure you will agree with me. There have been many days in my life when nothing less than my commitment to the ministry God gave me could keep me from quitting—quitting my job, quitting my responsibilities, quitting period! When discouragement that severe hits you, when you seem to be all alone, hang on to the promise you made. Your faithfulness to your promises will be the making of you! Whether anyone else stands with you, stand firm because God has asked you to and you have promised Him you would.

In Jerusalem and throughout the rest of his ministry, whether anyone else received him or not, Paul never swerved from his ministry. He must have nearly despaired at the fickleness of his weaker Christian brothers and sisters, but he persevered. In time, his steadfastness paid off. He found himself loving and being loved by hosts of worthy friends. That would not have happened to him if he had abandoned his calling.

When your eye is on your purpose in life and not on how life's treating you, you can ride out the lonely days and disappointing seasons. When you forget your mission, when resentment or bitterness creeps in because you think you are not getting your proper respect, you feel increasingly alienated. Loneliness is the direct result of too much thinking about yourself. If you are busy about your service, you can't afford the luxury of self-pity. You have too many other people to worry about. Nothing gets us out of our misery quite so quickly or thoroughly as being needed by someone.

President Franklin Roosevelt can give us some insight on this subject. Robert E. Sherwood in his *Roosevelt and Hopkins* records a conversation between Wendell Willkie and President Roosevelt in which the Republican candidate asked why the President kept Harry Hopkins as such a close advisor when so many people distrusted and resented him. Instead of taking offense at this personal question, Mr. Roosevelt told Mr. Willkie that if he were to become President one day, he would learn that almost everybody who walks through the Oval Office door wants something out of him. Then he would discover the value in a man like Hopkins, who wants nothing except the opportunity to serve you.

Because of Hopkins's desire to serve the President's needs, he enjoyed the full confidence and affection of the man he served. In the same way, when you as a servant of Christ want nothing more than to fulfill your ministry to the satisfaction of your Lord, you will also enjoy His loyalty and affection for you. It is another way of experiencing Christ's truth, "It is more blessed to give than to receive" (Acts 20:35). To give *without any thought of receiving* is especially blessed, because anything that is returned to you is an unexpected bonus.

Here, then, is the test. If you are battling loneliness, are you willing to serve Someone without expecting anything for your service except the privilege of serving? If you *are,* and if you *do,* then you *will* be blessed—and you will not remain lonely.

You Have Your Fellow Ministers

One of the special bonuses in ministry is the enjoyment of your fellow workers. You will in time develop the fellowship that comes to people who work together in a common cause. It is fun to eavesdrop at a veterans' reunion. They recall the danger, the misery, the stupid officers and the botched orders and the near misses and their friends who didn't make it. They are laughing and crying and bellyaching—and revelling in the special bond that ties men and women who have toughed it out together to win a battle.

That's the joy of fellowship in the Lord's army as well. My wife and I constantly thank God for our comrades in ministry. "We've been through the war together," we say of them. What we mean is this: we all lost ourselves in a cause that demanded everything we had to give. We certainly had no time to worry much about ourselves, or sometimes even about each other, but we all gave everything we had to fulfill our mutual ministry and the purpose for which the Lord called us together.

I am privileged to be a pastor on a large church staff. Several of us have now worked together for the better part of a decade. Along with them are a number of outstanding elders and other church leaders and members. Joy and I didn't know any of them when we first moved to Arizona. Now they are among our closest friends. No, we don't spend much non-working time together. No, we don't visit in each other's homes very often. No, we don't even chat much about personal matters at work. But we have been through wars together, and we are "there" for each other. We are not lonely.

Let me pick on one of them to illustrate my point. I'll use Mark, our college pastor. Mark has been with the church several years now. I've told him that he's the kind of man I instinctively dislike: very tall, quite handsome, gracefully athletic, with a winning personality and a gentleness of spirit that seem to come so naturally to him and are so unnatural to me. If I let myself, I could be quite envious.

Yet we are good friends. Our friendship didn't come about because one day in my loneliness I said to him, "Mark, I'm lonely. I'm going to make you my friend." I did not follow him around, making a nuisance of myself, in my earnestness to persuade him to take me on as a friend. Before long, even this gentle soul would have been tempted to give me the back of his hand. You don't make friends this way.

It wouldn't work. It wouldn't work because I wouldn't be thinking about Mark at all, but about myself and how I could get Mark to meet my needs. Mark and I are such good friends now because we never set out to become friends at all. We both simply signed on in the same army and were assigned the same regiment and have fought many battles side by side. Our commitment to ministry has made us friends.

When you join hands in serving the Lord, you won't be lonely, not for long, anyway, not if you are sincerely trying to please Him without worrying about your own popularity, and not if you do what you can to help your fellow ministers—without expecting anything in return from them.

I've kept two cartoons in my files for years. One shows a technician in a computer room. All the walls are filled with computers, this being back in computers' infancy. The man is on the telephone. The caption reads, "I'm lonely." Of course he is. Machines don't talk back; you cannot have fellowship with them.

The other one is simply a picture of a guy with a very sad face and a little balloon overhead in which you can read his thoughts. In this balloon is a Post Office "Man Wanted" poster of this same man looking out through bars, only this one reads, "Unwanted." You chuckle for a moment, then turn sober. There's nothing very funny about anyone's being unwanted.

You won't be, if you make yourself helpful. Here's my suggestion: pursue your ministry in a cause that allows you to work together with fellow ministers, making yourself useful and letting the relationships grow naturally—don't try to force them—out of your cooperating together to fulfill a ministry that is bigger than all of you.

It was ministry that brought Paul and Barnabas together and ministry that kept them together for their remaining years.

You Have Yourself

This last word almost seems to contradict the self-effacing humility that I seemed to be prescribing just now, but it doesn't. The truth is that people who have a healthy self-respect are seldom lonely. They are like a little girl I heard about, contentedly playing in her backyard sandbox. When a neighbor woman, seeing her by herself, asked her where her mother was, the girl said she was in bed, asleep. And her brother? He was taking his nap, too.

"Well, don't you mind being out there all alone, playing by yourself?"

"No," she said, "I like me."[3]

So did the apostle Paul. He would later write to his Philippian friends that even in the confines of prison he was content, as indeed he could be content in any situation (Philippians 4:11). Having discovered new life in Christ and trusting in a Source of power that could enable him to survive or even be triumphant in any situation (Philippians 4:13), he did not indulge in self-pity. He had no need to: he wasn't pitiful.

When you have accepted yourself as a child of God, you can learn to enjoy the company you're in, even if you are all the company you have.

How can you learn to like yourself? That's what this chapter has been all about. It's by getting your life right with the Lord, by enjoying His presence in your daily life, by accepting His call for you to give yourself generously in a ministry that's important in His kingdom on earth, and by yoking up with fellow ministers to get that job done that self-appreciation is developed. One truth you must fully grasp: you don't learn to like yourself by trying to. In that way lies futility. "For whoever wants to save his life will lose it, but whoever loses his life for me will save it" (Luke 9:24).

Is there anything more that needs to be said? Yes, and you have probably already thought of it. What about Jesus? He experienced rejection, didn't He? Yes. Abandoned by His friends, He even cried out on the cross, "My God, my God, why have *you* forsaken me?" There isn't anyone, then, even our Lord himself, who hasn't felt terribly alone.

Is my advice futile, then? No, because as Jesus' experience proves so conclusively, when He felt alone, He wasn't. His Father was near and His friends weren't far. He remained faithful to His ministry, even when He seemed to be the only one. The end of the story you know. He died and was resurrected. He forgot himself, and was remembered. He endured His loneliness, and is loved as no other person in history has been loved. He lost His life, and saved it.

---

[1]*Apologia pro vita sua,* 1968. Quoted in Ian Hunter, *Malcolm Muggeridge* (Nashville: Thomas Nelson, 1980), p. 12.

[2]Quoted in Leslie D. Weatherhead, *The Significance of Silence,* (Nashville: Abingdon Cokesbury, 1945), p. 54

[3]Joseph L. Felix, *Lord Have Murphy* (Nashville: Thomas Nelson, 1978), p. 136.

10
When Things Go Wrong
Acts 23:11-35; 2 Corinthians 11:24-33, 12:8-10

"There's little to tell you about me. It's summed up best, I think, by what I've said before, 'I'm sure the Lord loves some people; but then there are the rest of us.' I have and continue to have many problems...." With these doleful words, my correspondent brought her letter to a close. She truly does have many problems.

So do we all. Does that place us among "the rest of us"? Do our troubles signify that the Lord doesn't love us?

I don't know of anybody who had more problems than the apostle Paul had. I was reading Acts 23:11-35, the account of the plot against his life in Jerusalem, when I realized how very typical of his eventful life it was for him to be in such danger. Is this yet more proof that the Lord didn't love him? Look at this list of troubles from 2 Corinthians 11:24-33:

Five times I received from the Jews the forty lashes minus one.
Three times I was beaten with rods,
once I was stoned,
three times I was shipwrecked
I spent a night and a day in the open sea,
I have been constantly on the move.
I have been in danger from rivers,
in danger from bandits,
in danger from my own countrymen,
in danger from Gentiles;
in danger in the city,
in danger in the country,
in danger at sea;
and in danger from false brothers.
I have labored and toiled and have often gone without sleep;
I have known hunger
and thirst

and have often gone without food;
I have been cold
and naked.

Besides everything else, I face daily the pressure of my concern for all the churches. . . .

In Damascus the governor under King Aretas had the city of the Damascenes guarded in order to arrest me. But I was lowered in a basket from a window in the wall and slipped through his hands.

If your test of the Lord's love is whether or not you are free from troubles, then you have to conclude that Paul was indeed unloved. Things often obviously went wrong for him.

Not so long ago, one of the prominent members of our church told me that he became a Christian seven years ago. Following his conversion, he says, he has experienced the seven worst years of his life. It has sometimes seemed that everything has gone wrong. I asked him, then, whether he regretted his conversion and would like to return to his old life. "No way!" he exploded. "Christ has made all the difference in my life."

There you have it. He still has troubles, maybe even more than ever, but he wouldn't give up Christ for anything. For him it has been almost as if, when you accept Christ as Lord, you invite trouble.

That was certainly the case for Paul, wasn't it?

What about us? What are we to think when things go wrong?

Things May Seem Worse Because We Have Been So Comfortable

I've been concerned about our children. Not just my own, but all of my children's generation who have grown up in comfortable middle-class American homes. They've enjoyed an unprecedented period of prosperity. My children take for granted luxuries that my parents didn't dare dream of. If they have to cut back on their scale of living, it will be more difficult for them than for someone of my own or my parents' generation. When the living has been easy, then deprivation hits all the harder. What would we do without refrigerators or air conditioners (especially we Arizonans)? If we hit a financial reversal, will we conclude the Lord doesn't love us the way He loves some other people?

I like what Samuel Butler wrote in *The Way of All Flesh*. Referring to Jeremiah 31:29, "The fathers have eaten sour grapes, and the children's teeth are set on edge," Butler concludes that this isn't the problem so much as the fact that children of well-to-do parents suffer because their parents eat too many sweet ones. When parents indulge themselves in every comfort, they ill prepare their children for life's inevitable disappointments.

Christ never promised His disciples easy street. Most people in the world know that. Western Christians seem to be the exception. We have imbibed freely of the current heresy that equates material prosperity with God's blessings. We cheerfully conclude that our high standard of living is proof that God is smiling on us. Yet I can hardly think of a better way God could punish us as a nation than to let us become fat and sluggish in our prosperity. When other great nations before us did, they met their doom.

I'm afraid of this heresy. Its shallow arrogance is mind-boggling. With a flick of a backhand, it wipes out all Christians who have failed to prosper materially—victims of the Great Depression, victims of government mismanagement, victims of every economic reversal throughout history. How juvenile we sound to our Christian brothers and sisters suffering under totalitarian regimes.

Their perspective is much more like that of a proud Manchu woman that E. Stanley Jones tells about in his *Christ and Human Suffering*. She had steadfastly refused to become a Christian, in spite of all the appeals her believing friends and loved ones, including her husband, made to her. But when persecution broke out against the Christians and she and her husband had to flee for their lives into the mountains, where their sufferings were horrible, she converted. "Any religion that is persecuted this way must be true," she explained.[1] She was merely judging Christianity with the same measure Jesus used. Never once did He say, "Blessed are you when your bank account is full and you enjoy every luxury that this earth affords." To the contrary, He said, "Blessed are you when people insult you, persecute you and falsely say all kinds of evil against you because of me" (Matthew 5:11).

When Things Go Wrong,
They May Help Us to Hear God

I recently had a conversation with a man for whom this has just been proved true. He's middle-aged now. Life has really smiled on him. An independent businessman, he's prospered beyond his youthful dreams. But even as his business was growing and on the outside everything seemed to be prospering, he was inwardly rotting away. Tension wracked his home. His growing dependence on alcohol finally sent him to a rehabilitation center. That was followed by hospitalizations for two different physical problems. At the same time, his formerly passive teenage son was asserting himself—and getting in serious trouble in doing so.

Yet my friend has come through all these traumas with a strength of character that has me cheering for him. When he faced up to his alcoholism, he also faced up to his need for God. He now leans on the Lord as if his life depends on it, as of course it does. He confesses, though, that his post-conversion struggles have been the most difficult he has ever faced. I asked him, "Are you sorry you went in for treatment? Are you sorry that you gave your heart fully to the Lord?"

"Oh, no," he quickly protested.

"Would you go back?" I asked him.

"Never."

Then we talked about the meaning of joy, as opposed to happiness. Happiness depends on what "happens" to us, on things and events over which we have little control, but joy is a deep, abiding inner sense of peace and well being. It belongs to those who know they've "got it together" with God and they're "getting it together" with other people. He said, "Yes, that joy is what I've been experiencing—but I've sure been unhappy."

Again I asked him, "Would you trade it?" He must have grown tired of my asking him by now. "Of course not," he said, and that ended my probing.

Everything was going wrong, it seemed—but he was hearing God.

C. S. Lewis put it so well: "God whispers to us in our pleasures, speaks in our conscience, but shouts in our pains: it is His megaphone to rouse a deaf world!"[2] The famous missionary Hudson Taylor further aids our understanding: "It doesn't matter how great the pressure is; it only matters where the pressure lies—whether it comes between you and God, or whether it presses you near and ever nearer to His heart of love."[3]

There has always been pain, even in the Garden of Eden. Death was there, too. The birds that sang ate the worms that fed them. The trees in which the birds sang shed their dying leaves to feed soil from which the trees took their nourishment.

Pain has probably saved the race from physical extermination. Had there been no such thing as pain, we should probably not have survived as a race. For if we did not know that fire would cause pain to us if we thrust our fingers into it, we should probably let our fingers be withered by fire. If disease did not cause us pain, we should probably think little about it, and we should succumb to disease, because unwarned by pain. Pain says, "There is something wrong—attend to it." So pain turns out to be our friendly watchman guarding us against dangers to life. Pain is God's preventive grace, built into the structure of our physical life, to keep us from committing individual and collective suicide.[4]

So don't curse God when things go wrong. Let the pressure thrust you toward God so you can hear Him and correct your course.

When Things Go Wrong,
They Help Us to Hear and Help Other People

My recovering alcoholic friend, as he was talking with me, had difficulty speaking. Tears kept getting in his way. I've known him many years, and I don't think I'd ever seen him cry before. I asked him about it, because I wanted to offer a word of reassurance. Many of us Christian men have embarrassed ourselves with our tears—tears we didn't shed so freely before conversion. My friend had never before allowed anyone else, not even his wife or his children, to see him cry. He had built up his defenses so that no one could penetrate to the real man. Now he's vulnerable. He has admitted his sins and his hurts and his need for the Lord. For the first time in his life, he has allowed himself to feel the pain of others, especially those he has affected. Now when he looks into his wife's eyes, he can see the hurt that he put there. It's painful for him to look carefully at his children, because there, too, he sees what he has done. He is reaching out to them in ways that were not possible for him before, when he was hiding.

So he is now crying as he has never cried, because he cares as he has never cared. He has become a new person.

I think this is why Paul says here, "Who is weak, and I do not feel weak?" In his vulnerability, he identifies with all others whose weaknesses are like his. "Who is led into sin, and I do not inwardly burn?" His own sinfulness makes him one with them in their sin, and he regrets their error as he regrets his own.

His only boast is of his weakness. "If I must boast, I will boast of the things that show my weakness" (2 Corinthians 11:29, 30). Only in weakness—like his blindness on the road to Damascus, through which, for the first time, the truth about the Lord was able to penetrate Paul's consciousness—could the Lord use him. Only in insults, in hardships, in persecutions, and in difficulties could he stop struggling to be victorious through his own abilities and relax into the Lord's strength. And only because of his weakness could he sympathize and identify with others.

Josiah Royce, the philosopher, once said, "No man is safe unless he can stand anything that can happen to him." Missionary E. Stanley Jones once quoted Royce to a student, who thoughtfully responded, "Then not many of us are safe, are we?" Jones, retelling this incident in his autobiography, adds the incisive observation that the real follower of Jesus *is* safe, "for not only can he stand anything that can happen to him, but he can use anything that can happen to him."[5] This is the glory of the Christian life, isn't it? We are "more than conquerers through him who loved us" (Romans 8:37). The "more" is found in the fact that we not only can stand, but we can turn to profit for someone else whatever goes wrong.

Here I must become very personal. I have about decided that if I were to explain in a sentence the secret of my success as a minister, limited though it is, the explanation would be something like this: I have discovered myself to be thoroughly average. Average in what I have accomplished, average in what I have experienced, average in what I have suffered, and average in my disappointments.

You see, I intended to be far above average. Physically, I was not going to let myself become a typical pot-bellied, flabby-muscled, bifocalled, bushy-browed, seedy-dressed, snory-sleeping old man. Then I went and did it.

And when I married, one thing I knew for certain: I was not going to repeat the mistakes of a lot of husbands I knew. Pardon me if I don't elaborate here. Just let me say I've made my share.

As a parent? Well, of course, I certainly was going to be a distinct improvement over the parents I observed as a youngster. My kids, because of their superior upbringing, would be perfect. Well, I'm very proud of our children—but they aren't perfect. And frankly, that they turned out well is more in spite of, than because of, their father's contribution.

As a minister? Believe me, I was going to be a perfect minister if it killed me. And it nearly did. My trying wasn't enough.

In so many other ways I was going to be exceptional. I would be an astute manager of our money; never would I be guilty of investing our money in some flaky scheme. And I'm not going to—ever again.

I also dreamed that my family and I would escape the health problems that afflict others. We didn't escape those, either.

So here's my testimony. My family and I have drawn deeply of what life offers—all that's good and a lot that isn't. Unlike my correspondent, though, we haven't concluded that the things that have gone wrong prove that the Lord doesn't love us. We've turned out to be an average family, with average parents and average children, and I've turned out to be a pretty average minister with average gifts and average problems. This has been my greatest strength. Everything that has gone wrong I've been able to use to help somebody else.

In the beginning, I thought a minister had to live a perfect life and be the perfect example. Now I understand that if I had been able to escape the disappointments and heartaches of my life, I could not have served my people half so well. I wouldn't have understood. I couldn't have helped. I would not have been able to say, "I know. I've been where you are."

That's enough about me. What about you? What's gone wrong in your life? You have obviously been able to stand it, or you wouldn't be reading these words right now. You have come through. There's just one more question, though. Have you been able to use it for good? Has it helped you to help others? Who is benefiting from what you have suffered?

Have you discovered that when things went wrong in your life, you became more alert to how other people were feeling? Didn't your reversals make you a more sympathetic person? A deeper person? In fact, a richer one? Many of us don't really start to do right until things have gone wrong.

You won't benefit from your experiences, however, so long as your life is centered in yourself. If you are the center of your universe, then every cross word, every slight, every illness, and every disappointment will only deepen your resentment and hostility. But if you are living for the Lord, conscious of the fact that in His service your task is to live for others, lifting their spirits, helping carry their load, and giving them a reason to thank God, then everything that has gone wrong in your life can become a tool in assisting you to make things right in theirs.

Let me be specific. Widows have many opportunities to turn their grief into grace. A widow can sink back into her sorrow and hurt for herself, or she can step out of her self-pity and offer comfort to others who are bereaved. It hurts to lose a loved one. Admit it—then find someone who can benefit from what you have experienced.

Other singles have the same opportunity. It's so tempting for some unmarried persons, especially those who would rather be married, to pity themselves because they have been unable to secure a mate. It sometimes hurts to be single. Admit it—then find someone who can benefit from what you have experienced.

Right now, I have several friends in mind who have gone through severe financial reversals. It's painful to lose everything you have worked for. Yet I have seen these friends get up, shake off their blues, get to work to rebuild—and at the same time join hands with others in financial distress to encourage and assist them.

I could say similar things of some dear ones whose chronic illnesses have plagued them for years—and who are sources of inspiration and cheer to others to whom they reach out. They are hurting—but they are using their hurt to help others.

This, then, is the joy of the Christian life. You can *use* what goes wrong to the glory of God and to the development, if you please, of your own soul—and to the benefit of those whose lives your life touches. There hasn't been a liability in my life that God hasn't turned into an asset in my ministry: my parents' divorce, our family financial disaster, my own chronic illness, our marriage tensions, our children's storms and stresses--nothing has remained a negative. God has made all things positive.

When Things Go Wrong, They Make It Possible for Christ's Power to Rest on Us

"Therefore I will boast all the more gladly about my weaknesses, so that Christ's power may rest on me" (2 Corinthians 12:9).

What kind of power is this? In the Garden of Gethsemane, it seemed more weakness than power. On the cross, it appeared impotent. In the tomb, you'd have thought it was dead. What kind of power? It's nothing less than the kind that raises the dead!

James Michener in his *Chesapeake* makes the astute observation that a sailing ship, "like a human being, moves best when it is slightly athwart the wind, when it has to keep its sails tight and attend its course."[6] I've tried sailing a few times, and I know Michener is right. If the wind comes from directly behind the boat, pushing it forward, you can hardly control it and you shove along sloppily, going where the wind wants you. You are tempted to relax, because you are going somewhat in the direction you want, but before you know it, you have drifted off course. The wind's will prevails. "What is needed," Michener adds, "is a wind slightly opposed to the ship, for then tension can be maintained, and juices can flow and ideas can germinate, for ships, like men, respond to challenge."

What kind of wind? A police officer I know was falsely accused of serious felony. His career was threatened, his reputation severely damaged. He became deeply depressed, he was angry with his accusers and everybody else, and each day became a torture. Yet it was this experience that brought him back to Christ and a new life.

What kind of wind? A couple in their late thirties gave up on their stormy marriage. She filed for divorce. It was the shock that woke her husband from his stupor. They are now remarried, newly committed to Christ, and effectively evangelizing their friends who have seen their transformation. Their minister estimates that in the year of their remarriage, forty percent of the new members of his church came because of them.

What kind of wind? One family who only four years ago went through bankruptcy has helped countless others fight their way to financial recovery through job counseling, encouragement, and example.

What kind of wind? I've written before of a friend who went to jail for embezzlement. There he rediscovered himself, his loved ones, and his true relationship with the Lord. He calls his incarceration the best year of his life.

A wind "slightly opposed," forcing the best from us, causing us in our weakness to call on God's strength. That kind of wind.

"I'm sure the Lord loves some people; then there are the rest of us. . . ." My correspondent is wrong. She's not asking, "How can I make use of what has gone wrong to help other people?" Instead, she is enjoying her self-pity. In that way lies defeat. Remember Dr. Jones? "The Christian can use anything that happens to him."

Anything.

---

[1] E. Stanley Jones, *Christ and Human Suffering* (New York: Abingdon Press, 1933), p. 121.

[2] Roger Lancelyn Green and Walter Hooper, *C. S.: Lewis, a Biography* (New York: Harcourt, Brace and Javanovich, 1974), p. 187.

[3]Quoted in James S. Stewart, *River of Life* (Nashville: Abingdon Press, 1972), p. 59.

[4]E. Stanley Jones, *Victorious Living* (New York: Abingdon Press, 1936), p. 233.

[5]*A Song of Ascents* (Nashville: Abingdon Press, 1968), p. 183.

[6] James Michner, *Chesapeake* (New York: Random House, 1978), p. 445.

11
A Handicap to Boast Of
2 Corinthians 12:7-10; Acts 27; Romans 8:28

This is a subject I have thought about most of my life. I grew up feeling handicapped, and not for the reasons most of my friends think. Since I laugh so much about being somewhat diminutive of stature, they would immediately name my shortness as my handicap. They are mistaken. What they don't realize is that we Lawsons think that's an asset, not a liability.

No, my problem was asthma. It was as much a psychological as a physical handicap to a boy in my hometown, where it seemed to me that masculinity was defined by athletic prowess. My inferiority feelings were intensified by the fact that my father, who was much smaller than I, was a fine athlete, and I always felt I was a disappointment to him because I couldn't compete. Baseball, football, basketball, and even swimming demanded more lung power than I could predictably summon into service. I turned to music and drama as compensations. I have often since thanked God for the circumstances that led me to develop in these and other disciplines. But in a high school that seemed to idolize its athletes, these seemed to be poor, poor substitutes.

When I grew older, what had been a physical problem turned for a while into a spiritual problem because of a number of well-meaning but misguided Christian friends who said, "If you had enough faith, God would heal you." Prodded by this rebuke, I began quiet study of faith healing. When a certain still-famous healer came to town, I went to his services—and saw that not everyone was healed. My critical mind observed the difference in tone in the meeting between when the television cameras were rolling and when they weren't.

It isn't that I don't believe we can be healed by faith. I do. I fervently believe the church is in the healing business. It is just that I have discerned that not everybody who wants to be healed is. I have also observed that some of our most prominent "faith healers" have in more recent years begun to speak more apprecia-tively of conventional medicine. One of them has even built a hos-pital. By the way, it can't heal everybody, either.

Another observation, not very profound, is that sooner or later everybody, even those who have been healed at some time, dies. Obviously, then, in God's economy there is a place for death and, necessarily, for sickness that leads to death.

This takes me back to my youth. Why wasn't I healed? Was it because I didn't have enough faith? Was it because I asked incor-rectly? Or could it be that God had another answer for me?

His answer to me was already given to another, two thousand years ago. No other words of Scripture have helped me more in coping with chronic health problems than the one about Paul's "thorn in the flesh." I like to couple it with two others: the account of Paul's shipwreck and suffering aboard ship enroute to Rome (Acts 27), and the life-principle he formulated because of his chronic (health) and critical (shipwreck) problems: "And we know that in all things God works for the good of those who love him, who have been called according to his purpose" (Romans 8:28). The outline of this chapter comes from 2 Corinthians 12, but you will hear overtones of the other passages throughout.

Handicapped

Reading 2 Corinthians 12:7-10 one day, I had to stop as a new thought possessed me. This Paul, the great *apostle* Paul, the man whom some scholars have so admired that they refer to him rather than Jesus as the founder of Christianity, this man whom God used so mightily, was handicapped! I know that some interpreters have tried to explain that his "thorn" wasn't really a physical malady but something like persecution by the Jews or temptation. Maybe, but I doubt it. I am convinced that he refers to a physical impediment. There have been lots of guesses: epilepsy, perhaps, or maybe chronic ophthalmia (eye disease), or a speech impediment, or recur-ring malaria or Malta fever. We don't know what it was, but we do know that Paul suffered enough from it to beg the Lord to remove it. He didn't.

Paul calls it a "messenger of Satan." This "messenger" can be-come an instrument of God's grace. (As can a shipwreck—remem-ber Acts 27 and Romans 8?) We have learned enough of the Lord's providence in this book so far to be certain that God can turn any liability into an asset. I can testify with Paul that God is able to help us accomplish more in life through incompleteness than do many who boast of whole bodies and easy sailing.

Beethoven comes to mind. Considered one of Western civilization's greatest musicians, Beethoven struggled in his later years to continue composing in spite of his growing deafness. Instead of giving up, he learned to "hear" himself compose by clenching a stick in his teeth and holding it against the sounding board of the piano to detect the faint sounds. You can't help sympathizing with this artistic genius who could imagine such sublime music, but couldn't hear it. He said if he could only be rid of his affliction, he could embrace the world.

Beethoven's biographers have often mused on the contribution his deafness made to his gigantic accomplishment. Having to compensate for this handicap, he reached beyond his isolation to grasp inspirations that had never before been experienced. Beethoven's music is a gift he gave us, not in spite of, but because of, his "thorn."

If I were to speak of all of history's greats who reached their heights in spite of severe handicaps, this book could not contain them all. There is hardly a sound body to be found among the world's famous achievers. In the field of literature alone, one rarely meets a healthy writer. Consider John Milton's blindness, Alexander Pope's grotesquely deformed body, John Keats' and Emily Bronte's tuberculosis, Emerson's and Tennyson's battles with chronic infections, Flaubert's epilepsy, and psychological, economic, and social illnesses without end. Heinrich Heine spoke for them all:

Out of my deepest sorrows,
I make my little songs.

Dr. Samuel Johnson, the literary dictator of eighteenth-century London and author of our first important dictionary of the English language, battled childhood illnesses that left him half-deaf and half-blind. He suffered recurrent episodes of near insanity. He had to drop out of Oxford University because of his poverty. He married a woman twenty years his senior who died a bedridden addict. His prodigious labors to produce his literary masterpieces would have exhausted a lesser man, and the numerous times he was cheated out of his just recompense would have maddened almost anyone else. Yet his biographer W. Jackson Bates praises Johnson as "a heroic, intensely honest, and articulate pilgrim." So great was his triumph over his problems that Dr. Johnson is still required reading wherever English literature is taken seriously.

When I was a student, we still talked about Demosthenes, the great Greek orator. More than anything else, he wanted to help his country in its time of peril. The most effective way to do so, he believed, was through oratory. He made up his mind that he would become the most effective orator possible. That was no small goal for Demosthenes, because he stammered. Not one to be turned aside by an affliction, however, he wrote his own self-improvement program. He placed pebbles from the sea in his mouth and shouted against the noise of the waves. He overcompensated. He became one of history's greatest orators not in spite of, but because of, his handicap.

The poet Wordsworth said that he got much of his inspiration for writing at night. In order not to lose what he received, he taught himself to write in the dark. This is what I've been talking about: writing in the dark, learning to achieve even in the blackness, when times are most discouraging. When the pain is most intense, we stand to gain the most from it.

We have a greater obstacle to overcome than any handicap or pain: we must conquer comfort. Our addiction to ease is a huge impediment to success. There is no stimulation in comfort.

A certain student had made up his mind that he wanted to improve his intellectual life. He began by transforming his room into a study. He moved in a fine, overstuffed chair. He placed some slippers beside the chair and bought a handsome lounging jacket to keep himself warm as he studied. He affixed a special book rest on the arm of the chair and properly placed a reading lamp so that the light could shine directly on the book. He also put near the chair a swivel bookcase so that, while sitting in his chair, he could reach his books without having to get up. With everything in place, he would take off his shoes and put on his slippers and lounging jacket, ease himself into his chair, turn on his light, open his book, and promptly fall asleep.

Christian ministers will tell you that the biggest enemy of church growth and productivity is their members' dedication to comfort. In my church, we have no shortage of talent; God has collected here an amazing army of abilities. There is not even a lack of money, although it usually seems to be in short supply. We certainly don't want for opportunities; we can't take advantage of all the ones the Lord gives us. Our great handicap, though, is that too many of our members are comfortable. They don't want to be bothered. While the world is charging pell-mell toward Hell, some Christians are resting comfortably.

The result is that most ministers have to rely on people who are hurting or have been hurt. They'll do the work of the church because they care. When I need someone to show compassion and assist the needy, I never think to myself, "Now who has the leisure or the money to help?" I turn instead to someone who has experienced tragedy or is overcoming a handicap, someone whose heart has been broken. This person isn't too comfortable to care.

Arizona runs a lottery. I am constantly astonished at the money people throw away on it, hoping against incredible odds of winning a fortune. (The chance of winning our lottery is about as good as the chance of being struck by lightning.) I discovered that a member of my family bought a ticket. I've been praying for my children in a way they probably don't appreciate: "May nobody I love ever win the lottery!" Good luck is not what people need. I have never known good luck to build good character, but I have seen many, many people of good character manufacture their own good luck. I can't help wondering how much love and courage there would be in a world in which everybody was lucky.

Is it, then, so terrible to be handicapped?

Disappointed in Prayer

Another reason that Paul's experience with his "thorn" has been so helpful to me is that he didn't get what he prayed for.

Earlier in my life, when I was still praying for perfect health, I was confused because God did not take away my asthma. You can understand how comforting it was to read, "Three times I pleaded with the Lord to take it away from me . . ." and He didn't. "Lord, I want to be well. Lord, I could do so much more for you if only you would make my body work right." Did you ever pray like this? Did He give you what you wanted? Or did He answer you as He answered Paul: "My grace is sufficient for you, for my power is made perfect in weakness" (2 Corinthians 12:9). The "thorn" remained in his side; "the ship struck a sandbar and ran aground," and "the stern was broken to pieces by the pounding of the surf" (Acts 27:41). Paul was not strong enough to cast out his physical impediment nor to call off the storm that wrecked the ship. In both cases, however, God took care of him. It was as if He said to Paul, "The grace with which I saved you, the grace with which I called you to ministry, is the grace with which I will sustain you. You'll experience My power because of your weakness."

A compassionate minister once said that he often did not know how to speak to God when his people asked for him to intercede for them in their illnesses. He perceived their suffering doing so much good for their souls that he feared to ask the Lord to cure them. I identify with his dilemma. There is no proof that good health and good things in life produce good people.

Madeleine l'Engle, author of so many delightful books for children and adults, suffered her first attack of iritis, a little-known eye disease, when she was nine or ten. The next year she was attacked again. The doctor told her mother, in Madeleine's presence, that a third bout would cost her her vision. For the rest of her life, Miss l'Engle has lived in the shadow of blindness. The effect, however, has been to sharpen her vision and enhance her verve for living. She has seen more and seen it brighter than if she had never had iritis.

Her story recalls for me the day I was dashing across the street at nigh noon in downtown Indianapolis. A car struck and sent me flying through the air "with the greatest of ease." I landed abruptly, breaking my arm and nose and causing other assorted discomforts. The damage should have been much worse. I could just as easily have been killed. To this day, when I say, "I'm glad to be here," I want you to know I mean it! That near-fatal accident changed me, deepened my faith, and enriched my appreciation of life, although I still bear on my body the marks of my misadventure. I am not quite whole physically, yet it was good for my soul.

We can't leave this subject without remembering Helen Keller, can we? I can't imagine anything worse than being unable to see and hear, yet Ralph Barton Perry, in his forward to Miss Keller's autobiography, chides the readers for thinking of her primarily in terms of what she lacked. She could still experience nature, history, and society. She could touch, smell, and taste her world. The whole range of human emotions was hers, and with her fingers, she would read other people's moods on their faces. She had her mind, and a rich one it was, capable of thinking, comparing, remembering, anticipating, associating, imagining, speculating, and feeling. Of herself, Miss Keller wrote, "As time went on my thoughtless optimism was transmuted into that deeper faith that weighs the ugly facts of the world, yet hopes for better things and keeps on working for them even in the face of defeat."[1] How often she must have prayed, in her youth, to have her "thorn" removed. Yet think of what she—and we—would have missed if her request had been granted. Her life has taught us to probe more deeply. Instead of inquiring, "What have you lost?" we must ask, "What remains?" and, "What are you doing with it?"

This has special relevance for older adults, doesn't it? I have reached the age when every now and then my body tells me I have reached the age! People of my vintage have bodies that don't work as well as they used to. Among my contemporaries, when something breaks, you're pretty certain it can't ever be fixed quite right again. No use fighting it. Wishing doesn't help, either. You can't turn the clock back. Neither will cursing God for building you this way make anything better. So what are you going to do about your condition?

Start here: "My grace is sufficient for you." Accept the Lord's grace and accept aging as an expression of His grace. When you are in touch with the Lord, you realize that each chronological plateau has its own blessings. When you were young, you had a most "physical" existence. Your body was at its best, but your mind, emotions, and spiritual dimensions were badly underdeveloped. Truthfully, you were more handicapped then than now, at least in the things that matter most. It's only when you can't do what you'd like to do with your body that you discover those other elements of your being that enrich life to the fullest. What a glorious, wonderful day it is when a person stumbles on to this heretofore hidden fact: "I have a mind!" Another wonderful day: "I am a soul, created for eternity." Yet another: "A truly wealthy person counts his assets in friends, not dollars." When you make discoveries like these, you want to live life at a deeper, less physical level.

Then you realize that there is grace in sickness, grace in physical disability, grace in aging. You further come to know that there may be grace in success, but there is also—and perhaps more often—grace in failing to achieve a certain goal. You understand that those impediments in your physical being against which you used to curse and kick have become God's means of showering more grace upon you.

When I was young, I so badly wanted to play ball, but I couldn't, so I played the piano. To the kids in the neighborhood and at school, I was a sissy (or so I thought). But now my contemporaries can't play ball anymore, and I'm still playing the piano. I couldn't run far in those days, so I read books instead. I couldn't sing, so I acted. Every time the door was shut because of this or that inadequacy in me, another one was opening for which I was qualified. Now I realize that it is not in spite of my handicaps that life has been so rich for me, but because of them. His grace has been sufficient.

Listen to Jesus, praying in Gethsemane: "My Father, if it is possible, may this cup be taken from me" (Matthew 26:39). It wasn't taken. Hear Him on the cross: "My God, my God, why have you forsaken me?" He hadn't been forsaken. God was reaching and teaching us through Christ. What seemed momentarily to be Christ's defeat—and it was a terrible thing to die on a cross—was instead the darkness before the light, the storm before the calm, the death that leads to life.

We think only a yes answer to our prayers counts. These Scriptures help us realize that we will sometimes be disappointed in our requests, because God wants to demonstrate His power for our good through our disabilities. You may still wheeze, even after asking God to cure you. Then you must ask, "All right, Lord, if I'm still going to wheeze, what do you want to do through my wheezing?" So whether you eat or drink or even wheeze, "do it all for the glory of God" (1 Corinthians 10:31).

Boastful in Christ

And if you boast, "boast all the more gladly about [your] weaknesses, so that Christ's power may rest on [you]" (2 Corinthians 12:9). Will you forgive me if I become personal one more time? I have occasionally thought about what would have become of me if I had been given the perfect body I prayed for. I know one thing for certain: if God had given me the Charles Atlas body I dreamed of, I probably would not have had nearly so much fun. I certainly wouldn't have laughed as much. I might have developed some vanity about my good looks, and vain people can't laugh at themselves. In this simple way, I have learned what Paul speaks of here. If I am going to boast, it will not be of my physical attributes. He means, "When I am weak, then I am strong. When I don't seem to have anything to boast about, then I can be used."

Yehuda Bacon, an Israeli sculptor imprisoned in Auschwitz as a young boy, said that when he was still in the prison, he thought he would tell people what he saw in the concentration camp in the hope that people would change for the better. Later, as an adult, he learned to his dismay that people didn't want to change and didn't even really want to know what he had learned in his suffering. Only much later did he comprehend that suffering has meaning only for the sufferer, and then only if it changes him for the better.

We speak much of Jesus' suffering, but His suffering remains meaningless for us unless we let it change us. The chances are that we won't until we have experienced some handicap or shipwreck or other form of suffering ourselves. Then His power can rest on us and work through us.

E. Stanley Jones was speaking one day in China on this very subject. In front of him he saw a badly crippled little lady. She was so deformed that she couldn't see over the back of a bench. He prayed for her as he spoke, hoping she would derive some comfort from his words. He was wasting his sympathy. She had something to teach him.

After his speech, a lady missionary introduced him to the little crippled lady as one of the mission's best teachers. "She is the greatest spiritual power in this school, and has led more people to God than any other person in this city," she added.

Her story inspired Dr. Jones. As a child, she had been dropped. The fall broke her back. She grew into a bad-tempered, sharp-tongued, bitter woman, trapped in her pitifully deformed shell. Then one day, she let Christ take over her life, and He transformed her. She studied to become a teacher.

When she was sent to a certain village to take charge of the school there, the villagers almost rioted in protest. They superstitiously thought her crippled body a bad omen. The missionary stood by her, though, and the villagers finally relented out of pity. Several years later, when the mission moved her to a larger school elsewhere, the villagers nearly rioted again—this time to keep her.[2] God had used her mightily. Her bent body became the instrument of His grace.

I suspect that when she was young, she often prayed for a better body. He didn't give her one. Instead, He helped her become a beautiful person. Through her weakness, her beauty could shine for the Lord.

I hope you haven't misunderstood me in this chapter. I believe in healing that removes thorns from sides; I believe in miracles that calm the storms at sea. There have been too many affirmative answers to prayer in my life to have any doubt about God's ability to work miracles. But this chapter is for people like me who are still wheezing or hurting, whose bodies are less than perfect. Please don't despair. You didn't pray wrong. It isn't your lack of faith that's at fault, any more than Paul's. You and Paul and I just belong to the company of saints through whose weakness God will let His strength flow. God will use us to help others, if we will let Him.

Maybe your role in life is like mine. I can't stand before my congregation and impress them with my perfectness. No, my role is to enable them to say, "Well, if God can do something with a person in that shape, maybe He'll do something with me."

Not in spite of, but because of.

_____

[1]*The Story of My Life* (New York: Doubleday and Company, 1902), pp. 15, 16.

[2]*Christ and Human Suffering* (New York: Abingdon Press, 1933), pp. 95-97.

12

Strength to Overcome Temptation
1 Corinthians 10:12, 13; Ephesians 6:10-18

One of my favorite *Peanuts* strips shows an insomniac Snoopy vainly trying to get some sleep on top of his doghouse. It isn't working. Disturbing sounds are wafting his way from the house. Finally he gives up, tromps to the door, bangs on it ferociously, and delivers his complaint to Charlie Brown. After careful investigation, Charlie Brown returns to tell Snoopy he was right. The lid was off the cookie jar. A now contented beagle returns to his rooftop, musing that no one can sleep with a bunch of chocolate chip cookies singing all night.

Temptation. Just when you think you are making progress in your Christian growth, the Tempter sneaks up on your blind side and flattens you. A young man recently came to talk to me about his future plans. He gave his life to the Lord about four years ago. Since then, he has steadily matured in his walk with Christ, although he has often become discouraged because of his tendency to slip back to his old ways. He asked to see me, though, because just the week before, he and his wife had agreed that he should begin making serious plans to prepare for full-time Christian ministry. Then, he told me, he almost cancelled his appointment because it had been one of the roughest weeks he has had as a Christian. He was convinced that he was unworthy even to talk about ministry, after enduring such a bombardment of temptations. Obviously, he told me, somebody didn't want him to get so serious about serving the Lord.

Obviously. When you become a Christian, you are at that time joined in an ongoing battle of nerves with the Tempter. I often have reason to observe that immediately following Jesus' baptism, after the heavens were opened and the dove descended and the voice of God himself spoke a reassuring word, Jesus was driven into the wilderness to be tempted by the devil. We do not escape temptation when we become Christians; actually, it seems to intensify. No wonder the apostle Paul cautions, "So, if you think you are standing firm, be careful that you don't fall!" (1 Corinthians 10:12).

When you are young, you hope that when you grow up, some of your temptations, maybe all of them, will disappear. But when you are older, you discover that you have simply replaced ones peculiar to youth with others peculiar to maturity. You haven't escaped. Hormones attack us when we are young; urges, drives, and passions take charge to our frequent embarrassment. In our middle years, enticements of the body are supplanted by greed or power hunger or compromise. Even in old age we aren't safe. The problems then are a hardening of the attitudes, an increasingly judgmental spirit, and comforting doses of self-pity. A good spiritual exercise at any age is to memorize and then to pray these words with the Psalmist:

Search me, O God, and know my heart;
test me and know my anxious thoughts.
See if there is any offensive way in me,
and lead me in the way everlasting (Psalm 139:23, 24).

We must understand that temptation to be unfaithful is necessary before we can tell whether we are really being faithful or just untried. We can't be certain of our faith until we have been pricked by doubt. We certainly can't boast of our moral purity if we have never had anyone try to lure us into impurity. Some super-sensitive Christians carry loads of undeserved guilt because they have felt tempted. They expect better of themselves. They don't have any idea that they are chastising themselves for not being superior to Jesus, for even He was "tempted in every way, just as we are—*yet was without sin*" (Hebrews 4:15).

The human mind is capable of allowing any idea, even the most impious and the most criminal, to appear without any act of will on our part. The fault does not lie in its appearance, but only in our acceptance and enjoyment of it. Martin Luther used to say that we can't prevent birds from flying over our heads, but we can prevent them from building nests in our hair. It isn't the temptation, but the indulging of it, that gets us into trouble.

Watching a television video recently made all this very vivid for me. One of today's most popular comedians was on stage before a well-dressed audience of thousands. His language and subject were as vile and as foul as anything I've seen. He piled profanity on top of obscenity topped by vulgarity and served the mess with a garnish of verbal garbage. The lack of imagination in his language should have made an undergraduate blush, but he revelled in it. What bothered me most, though, was not his display of gutter humor, but the obvious delight and approval of his audience. They ate it up.

What once was confined to the locker room or clandestine behind-the-barn boyhood experimentation is now broadcast from the stage to "sophisticated" men and women from every walk of life and then recorded on videotape for replay in the politest of home parlors. It's a symbol of our culture. Temptation is on the air waves, invading living rooms, penetrating even "spiritual" consciousnesses. You can't escape, if you view television, read a newspaper, or subscribe to a secular magazine. The temptation to live at the level of our society is always present and quite appealing.

But "God is faithful; he will not let you be tempted beyond what you can bear. But when you are tempted, he will also provide a way out so that you can stand up under it" (1 Corinthians 10:13). That way is spelled out for us in Ephesians 6:10-18.

Believe and Tell the Truth

"Stand firm, then, with the belt of truth buckled around your waist" (Ephesians 6:14). Let me state this truth as straightforwardly as I know how. If you are sincere about wanting to succeed in overcoming temptation, if you will make yourself a promise ahead of time, before you have to make the decision, this one promise will save you all kinds of grief: "I will under all circumstances tell the truth." If you sincerely make this covenant with yourself, then you will not want to do anything that you will have to lie about afterwards. If you have to cover up your actions from your spouse or your children or your parents or your boss or anyone else (even the Internal Revenue Service), then you are in trouble. Make it an act of faith that you will be obedient to Jesus in letting your yes be yes and your no be no (see Matthew 5:37). Dare to become transparent—let your whole being be seen. You have nothing to hide. You don't have to live a lie.

Ephesians 4:25 speaks directly to this issue, doesn't it? "Therefore each of you must put off falsehood and speak truthfully to his neighbor, for we are all members of one body." We are also members of the body of Christ, who called himself "the way, *the truth,* and the life." In this, as in other important characteristics, we want to be like Him.

Do the Right Thing

"With the breastplate of righteousness in place" (Ephesians 6:14). This word *righteousness* bothers us a bit because it sounds so "churchy." It is a good term, though; it means being in the right relationship and doing the right things, right with God and right with people (and, for that matter, right with "things"). Once again, you can help yourself fend off temptation by deciding ahead of time that just as you will always tell the truth, you will also always do the right thing. This sounds almost childishly simple, doesn't it? You might be surprised, though, to know how many times someone has come to the minister for help with this confession: "Well, I knew at the time that I probably shouldn't be doing it, but I went ahead anyway." Then what could the person expect? He deliberately decided to do the wrong thing! Now he is suffering the consequences.

If I am right, Thy grace impart,
Still in the right to stay;
If I am wrong, oh teach my heart
To find that better way.

These noble lines from Alexander Pope's "Essay on Man" don't find nearly as ready reception in our wandering hearts as this all-too-truthful lament:

I do not know, I do not care
How far it is to anywhere;
I only know that where I'm not
Is always the alluring spot.

So we go to the alluring spot, "just to check it out," and before we know it, we're in trouble. As someone has truthfully said, "My problem is not lack of willpower; it's lack of won't power that gets me into trouble." Mark Twain has observed the same thing, commenting that "it's easier to stay out than to get out."

Yet we succumb, unconscious of the power we have to resist the lure, if we want to. We have been made righteous. God has graciously placed us in a loving relationship with himself. Christ saved us, brought us close to God, empowered us with the Holy Spirit, and even offered us a reward for seeking first the things of the kingdom of God (Matthew 6:33). Through the blood of Jesus

112

Christ, we've had our sins forgiven and our past washed away. All we have to do is act like it.

Share Your Good News

"With your feet fitted with the readiness that comes from the gospel of peace" (Ephesians 6:15).

Isn't this a descriptive phrase? It makes you think of that old Negro spiritual, doesn't it? "You got shoes, I got shoes, all God's chillun's got shoes." These, though, are special shoes. They are ready for walking with good news. Here's where we become discouraged, especially we parents. We pour out our best for our children, teaching them the finest we know, but then, when they reach the age of independence, they leave what we have taught them. They go exploring. And they break our hearts.

Why do they do this to us? Christian kids are often guilty of this sin against their parents partially because we have protected them. They have grown up in a sheltered environment. Mom and Dad have enjoyed a fairly stable relationship, family life is not bad, and lots of this world's enticements have been kept away. But the children know they are out there, and when freed to go exploring, they do. It seems to be much more exciting out there than in their dull if respectable homes. So we parents have to hang on during this period. We must be true to ourselves and to our standards, to our prayer life, and be constant in our love for our children. It's a risky time for them. More than they would ever admit, they need for us to be stable, for their sakes.

Parents, we don't need to despair. We still have something to offer our children. In the first place, we have survived. Second, we have some values to which we cling because we know their worth. Third, we have seen with Shakespeare that "all that glitters is not gold." We have chosen the Christian life-style because we have seen too much phoniness in this world. We want something that's for real, something permanent—something eternal.

We have found this good news in Jesus Christ, and our lives in Him have given us peace and joy. We know that the good life doesn't depend on drugs, on being "cool," on alcohol, on "getting ahead," or on power or fame or fortune. We have experienced peace—peace in the heart, peace with God, peace within the family, peace with friends, peace on earth and good will among men! We have nothing to be defensive about and every reason to assume the offensive and share this good news.

The best defense against temptation is a good offense. The best antidote to this world's bad news is eternity's good news.

Let Your Faith Defend You

"Take up the shield of faith, with which you can extinguish all the flaming arrows of the evil one" (Ephesians 6:16).

A shield is defensive armor. Defensive. We've turned things around, haven't we? For some reason, we believe it's the Christian's job to defend the faith. That's not right. Our faith defends us. It helps us to resist those seductions that could ruin us. There are times when we must say of some temptation, "No, I'm sorry. I can't do that. You see, I'm a Christian, and what you are proposing is just not an option for me." Of course, you will be laughed at—for a moment. But not for long. Even our jaded world admires people of conviction. Let your faith defend you.

There's a sad bit of Arizona history that helps us understand this principle. Every time I learn more of what the white man did to the Indians in this territory I live in, I want to weep. Back in 1785, the Spanish Indian fighter Bernardo de Galvez was appointed viceroy over the Indians out here. He devised the Galvez plan, which he entitled *Instructions for Governing the Interior Provinces*. He called for an all-out war on all Indians who refused to make peace with Spain. Those who did capitulate, however, were resettled in areas he called "establishments of peace." There the Indians were systematically weakened by debauchery in alcoholic beverages (supplied by the Spanish). The Apaches were also given old surplus firearms for hunting (replacement parts and ammunition supplied by the Spanish). These guns were not nearly as suitable for the Indians as their traditional bows and arrows, but they mistakenly valued them above their own weapons. The third element in the plan was to keep the tribes at war with each other while keeping them all friendly toward Spain. Amazingly, the subterfuge worked. The Indians' growing dependence on Spain and increasing hostility toward each other accomplished what Spain had been unable to achieve earlier with the cross or the sword.

The Indians rendered themselves defenseless. They believed the lies of the white man. They adopted his ways. They thought that because he was superior in firepower, he must be superior in all ways. They threw down the weapons that had defended them in exchange for foreign ways that made them helpless dependents.

114

Now it's the white man's turn. He has been deserting his traditional values as well, exchanging the faith of his fathers for the lies
of the Tempter, becoming increasingly dependent on guns and
goods controlled by his enemy. He has failed to learn the most
elementary lesson: you don't defeat your enemy by abandoning
your strengths and imitating his weaknesses.

You don't have to be defensive about your Christian faith. Don't
apologize for believing in the truth that sets men free. Your salvation has been and still is in Christ, whose Spirit will protect you like
a shield of faith, if you will let Him. But if you give up your faith
with its accompanying high ethics and Spirit-inspired strength, if
you become embarrassed by its other-worldliness and adopt the
ways of this world, you make yourself vulnerable by becoming
dependent on what will ultimately destroy you. The alternative is
clear: let your faith defend you.

I must say a word about the church here, about why I so fervently believe in it. The church expects something of me and gives
much more in return. The church is a body of people who
strengthen each other and are strengthened by the indwelling Holy
Spirit. Christians do not have to make their way alone through this
hostile environment. The Lord has bound us together, and together
we are strong.

Let your faith, and the communion of your fellow believers, be
your defense against the temptations of this world.

Relax in Your Salvation

"Take the helmet of salvation" (Ephesians 6:17).

If you have given your life to the Lord in obedient response to
His grace, you know that He has saved you. Relax in that knowledge. Enjoy your relationship. You don't want to go too far in your
relaxation, of course. You don't want to be like Judas, in whom
familiarity with the Lord seems to have bred contempt. He became
too casual, too impatient. He took the Lord too much for granted
instead of for example.

There will always be an element of alertness in our walk with
Christ. We are friends, but we are not equals. My word is not as
valuable as His; my opinion is not to be considered as important as
His. He is still Lord.

Remembering this truth can help us overcome the terrible, stressful, anxiety-producing gospel of our day: "I've got to be me." A
recent conversation with a woman who has claimed to be a

Christian for many years, but whose life-style directly violates many of Christ's explicit teachings, ended on this sour note. She loftily dismissed her sins with a wave of her hand and a toss of her head: "But I've got to be me."

No she doesn't. I don't either. Neither do you. You don't have to be you, thank God! You can be better. You can be what the Lord had in mind for you when He designed you. So relax. Trust His design. Trust His love for you. Be assured that He wants to save you and improve you. He won't let go of you until He has finished recreating you. Don't presume on His love, but enjoy it.

The problem with insisting on being you is that you (like me) are selfish. You are uptight. You are heading for trouble without the Lord. There are some things He insists you "gotta" be: You've got to be a Christian. You've got to be a child of God. You've got to be truthful. You've got to be loving. You've got to be saved.

A high order, one that you cannot fill no matter how hard you work at "being yourself" or even how hard you work at being the ideal Christian. But don't leave this truth out: He's going to help you do all of these things and more, if you will let Him. So relax. Put on the helmet of salvation. Trust your Savior to deliver you. He'll keep you safe.

Know God's Word

"And the sword of the Spirit, which is the word of God" (Ephesians 6:17).

Charles Swindoll was in Canada, away from home for eight days and facing a couple more there before he could return home. He was tired, he was lonely, and he was tempted.

He had finished his dinner in the hotel restaurant and was returning to his room through the lobby when he noticed a couple of attractive young women at the phone beside the elevator. He stepped into the elevator and they followed. He punched the button for the sixth floor, then asked them which floor they wanted. "How about the sixth floor?" they answered. "Got any plans?" The famous Charles Swindoll. In an elevator with two pretty, available young women. In Canada. His wife, his children, his church members, nowhere around. Who would ever find out?

It wasn't the thought of any of them that kept him honest, he says, but some Scriptures that God immediately gave him:

"Do not be deceived: God cannot be mocked. A man reaps what he sows" (Galatians 6:7).

"Put on the full armor of God so that you can take your stand against the devil's schemes" (Ephesians 6:11).

"In the same way, count yourselves dead to sin but alive to God in Christ Jesus. Therefore do not let sin reign in your mortal body so that you obey its evil desires" (Romans 6:11, 12).

So he told them, "No, thank you," and went to his room alone. He said they looked at him as if he were Mork from Ork, but he thanked God that His Word had come to him in that moment.[1]

Keep the Word of God and it will keep you in the moments when you most need it. When Jesus was tempted by the devil in the wilderness, he fended off Satan's thrusts each time with the Word of the Lord (see Matthew 4). Study your Bible. Know what God says. Be able to say with the Psalmist, "I have hidden your word in my heart that I might not sin against you" (Psalm 119:11).

Pray in the Spirit

"And pray in the Spirit on all occasions with all kinds of prayers and requests. With this in mind, be alert and always keep on praying for all the saints" (Ephesians 6:18).

Paul says "all" several times here. Prayer is not a hit-and-miss activity. It is constant. It is inclusive. We pray

"on all occasions"

"with all kinds of prayers and requests"

"always"

"for all the saints."

Let your life be saturated with prayer so that constantly you are aware of the presence of God. Being aware of His presence, there are places you will not go, activities you will not indulge in, language you will not utter, thoughts you will not entertain, temptations you cannot yield to. Praying all the time for all the saints will cure you of any notion that you live only for yourself. You can't pretend to be the "Lone Christian" while constantly praying for your brothers and sisters in Christ.

Pray all the time. Then you will be strong in the Lord.

----

[1] *Three Steps Forward, Two Steps Back* (New York: Bantam Books, 1980), pp. 100, 101.

13

When Death Visits You
Matthew 5:4; John 14:1-11

My one major fear when I became a minister was of funerals. I had no idea what I would say, couldn't imagine how I would say it, didn't even know what I should say. Further, there was no way of knowing when the first one would come nor whose it would be, so I couldn't prepare ahead of time.

It was just as well. I never could have guessed that my first one would be for Mary Smith. The call came at seven o'clock one morning. Mary had died at three. The day before, she was not feeling very well, so she took the day off from work. That evening, Ralph drove her to the hospital, and by eleven, the doctors had finished their diagnosis. Mary had acute leukemia. By three she was gone.

In his typically thoughtful way, Ralph waited until he was certain I would be awake before he phoned. I rushed to his house and was with him as one by one he had to tell his five children that their thirty-five-year-old mother was dead.

Scriptures came to mind, but they hardly seemed enough to ease the pain in this grieving family. Of course, I thought of Matthew 5:4, but it had always puzzled me and I wasn't certain in that moment that it made any sense at all: "Blessed are those who mourn, for they will be comforted." As each of the children came into the kitchen and their father had to break the sad news again, comfort seemed far away and any promise of blessing just hollow words. How helpless I felt as I prepared to leave when three-year-old Margaret asked me, "Are you going to get my mommy now?"

Nothing causes us to bemoan our helplessness like death, which touches us all. Even great theologians aren't exempt. Martin Luther, one of history's greatest Christian leaders, was as human as the rest of us when his fourteen-year-old daughter lay dying. "O God," he prayed, "I love her so, but Thy will be done." He reproached himself because he acknowledged that God had blessed him as no bishop had been blessed for a thousand years by giving him a wife and children, yet he couldn't find it in his heart to thank God at that moment. He held her in his arms as she died. "How strange it is to know that she is at peace and all is well, and yet to be so sorrowful."

In the face of death, our faith in the Lord bumps up against our strongest human emotions. We want to be able to sing, "It is well, it is well with my soul," but the words won't come.

It is now more than a quarter of a century since Mary Smith's death, and I have come to appreciate Jesus' words. It *is* blessed to mourn. Express Jesus' thought in the negative, and it becomes very clear: "Cursed is the person who cannot mourn, who has no one for whom to mourn, for such a person cannot be comforted." Blessed, indeed, are you when you care so much about another person that his or her passing leaves you feeling empty and bereft, for the alternative is terrible to consider—to have nobody to mourn for, nobody whose passing would leave you lonely, nobody who matters that much.

The death of any close loved one forces us to think long, long thoughts. We ponder the meaning of love, of friendship, of life itself. We confront our mortality. One day we shall not be mourning, but shall be the object of mourning. We shall die. How can we we sing "It Is Well With My Soul" when in the end we die? What comfort can we find in the Lord, when we know our end is inevitable?

You Don't Need to Be Afraid (John 14:1, 7-11)

Jesus answers our questions in the fourteenth chapter of John's Gospel, as He is preparing His disciples for His own imminent death on the cross. "Do not let your hearts be troubled," He tells them. "Trust in God; trust also in me." He explains in the seventh verse why they can have confidence in Him: "If you really knew me, you would know my Father as well. From now on, you do know him and have seen him."

That isn't sufficient for Philip. "Lord, show us the Father and that will be enough for us."

Jesus seems a little vexed as He replies, "Don't you know me, Philip, even after I have been among you such a long time? Anyone who has seen me has seen the Father. How can you say, 'Show us the Father'?" Philip, you've heard Me teach, you've seen My miracles; surely you understand by now that the Father and I are one.

Surely you must know that I speak with the authority of God himself. Trust Me, Philip. You don't have to be afraid.

Jesus is not offering His disciples the comfort of words alone, just a detailed description with accompanying promises of the hereafter. He does something far better. He offers himself. "I have walked among you, I have talked with you, fed you, and performed miracles for you as signs of My authority. You have seen My power at work. You have learned you can have confidence in Me, so trust Me. Believe *in Me* when I tell you that there is hope beyond the grave. You don't have to be afraid."

Trust didn't come easy for His disciples, and it comes with even more difficulty today. In a recent flight from London, the extent to which ours has become a suspicious, paranoid society was made painfully clear. I departed for New York's Kennedy Airport from London Heathrow. After checking in and receiving my boarding pass, I made my way past passport control and started through security control. My carry-on luggage rode on the conveyor belt through the X-ray machine while I walked through the electronic scanning device that scrutinized me for any sign of a concealed weapon. I stepped over to the belt to retrieve my travel bag just as a security guard whisked it away to another table, where she methodically looked into every dark nook and potential cranny. My first thought was that something strange must have appeared on the screen as it went through the X-ray machine, but I was wrong. Every passenger's bag was being searched a second time. This double-check is strange, I thought. But security wasn't finished with me yet.

When my flight was called, I made my way down one of those almost interminable Heathrow corridors to enter the lounge at the announced gate. Before I could enter, though, I had to make my way through a gauntlet of at least six more security guards. I was sent to the third one from the other end, and once again my hand luggage was thoroughly searched, and a male guard searched my body quite completely. I couldn't be offended, because there was nothing personal in this excessive precaution. Terrorism was rampant in the world, and the airlines were doing everything in their power to keep their passengers safe. In the process, they didn't dare trust anyone, even me, a substantial citizen and a nice person besides. They were afraid.

If you apply for a job in a large corporation, you may very well be required to take a psychological test to determine whether you are sane, a polygraph test to see whether you are honest, and may even be asked to offer a urine sample to learn whether you use drugs or not. Why don't they just ask you these things? Because they don't trust you. As a society, we've proved ourselves untrustworthy, and where there is no trust, there is fear. So the adolescent complains to his parents, "You don't trust me," and his parents don't. In a household in which people have reason to disbelieve in one another, suspicion and fear prevail.

To our paranoid age, then, Jesus says, "You don't have to be afraid. You can trust Me." We want to have confidence in Him, yet even longtime Christians hear Him tentatively. I was recently speaking with a fine Christian couple in their sixties. They had been planning to visit their son and daughter-in-law and grandchild in Europe, but with the recent terrorist activity in several European cities, they were having serious second thoughts about the trip. They were afraid.

Why should they be? They have lived a good life, they have served the Lord with honor, and they say they have placed their lives in His safekeeping. Of what should they be afraid? Of death? But if they should die, isn't there a place for them in Heaven?

These good people reminded me of another good person, a young woman I knew years ago who frequently talked of her faith in tones that from anyone else would have sounded like boasting. In spite of her protestations of great trust in the Lord, however, you should have been with us as we were driving through the mountains of North Carolina in a snowstorm. She was petrified. She was certain that we'd all be killed. Had I said anything, she would have protested that her faith was in the Lord and not in my driving. Suppose, however, we *had* all been killed. What then? Isn't there a place prepared for us? And don't we like to testify that Heaven will be far, far better than this world? So what's to fear?

"Do not let your hearts be troubled. Trust in God."

"Trust also in me."

It's good that we have this instinct for self-preservation. God put it in us. It is also good to exercise prudence in the conduct of our affairs. We should not tempt fate by flinging ourselves about foolishly. But it is not good to proclaim a faith in the Lord on the one hand while cowering in fear of death on the other. "Trust in me."

Catherine Lamb, a dear friend and sensitive poet, sent me this simple poem about her mother's fear of death and her surprise ending:

I can't forget, when Autumn comes,
how sad she used to be,
to see the shadows lengthen
and the leaves turn on the tree.
"It is a melancholy season,"
she would say, with heavy sighs.
And I'd catch a fleeting shadow
flash an instant in her eyes.
All her life she dreaded Autumn
and looked forward so to Spring.
She had no premonition
of what Spring would one day bring.
For it was not in Autumn's golden
days, that she had dreaded so,
But in the gladness of the Springtime,
that she was called to go.

Don't be afraid. You know neither the season nor the hour when you will die. Don't rob yourself of today's beauty because you dread a storm tomorrow. You must not miss autumn's beauty because you fear it is the season of your departing. Enjoy it until you go. When you are in Christ, you have nothing to fear.

There Is a Place for You (John 14:2)

"In my Father's house are many rooms; if it were not so, I would have told you. I am going there to prepare a place for you." I memorized this verse first from the King James Version, which reads, "In my Father's house are many mansions...." My visual imagination had trouble fitting those palaces into a house. I didn't know then that "mansions" in King James' English merely meant "dwelling place." Jesus is just offering assurance that in Heaven, there is a place for us.

His language is a rebuke to ours, isn't it? When someone dies, we speak of the "dear departed one"; we should talk instead of the one who has arrived. Another dear friend, Ernest Chamberlain, is now in his seventies. Unlike many people who flippantly speak of the day they'll be "checking out," Ernie speaks of how close he is to "checking in." There's a place for him.

I was touched by the young boy who stopped talking when his grandfather died. His older brothers and sisters thought he was quite calloused when he didn't join in their mourning, but his mother knew better. That night she heard him struggling through his prayer. When he came to the "God bless" portion, he stopped. He tried again, and stopped. Finally on the third try, he made it. "And God, please take care of grandfather wherever you want him to be—another star or wherever you think and make him be all right and we love him. Amen." He trusted God to give his grandfather a place.[1]

I read of a woman in Massachusetts who faithfully visited her husband's grave plot in the St. John the Baptist Cemetery every week for seventeen years. When the family decided to move his remains to a larger family plot, she gave instructions and the cemetery workers dug him up. They discovered to her horror (she was there, making certain everything was done right) that while she had been praying at plot #129, her husband reposed in plot #126. She sued the cemetery for a quarter of a million dollars for the emotional trauma she endured after this discovery. That is how important having the correct "place" was to her.

A burial plot isn't the place Jesus is talking about, though. He is referring to our eternal home. A Christian's assurance of a final Heavenly "resting place" makes us quite casual about where our physical remains lie. Heaven is our destination. You may pray for me at plot #126 or plot #129 or at no plot at all. Nobody is there. The place prepared for us is not in the cold earth but in the warm light of the everlasting Son. Jesus calls himself "the way and the truth and the life" and declares that "no one comes to the Father except through me" (John 19:6). Several times in the Gospel of John, Jesus claims a remarkably exclusive relationship with His Father. He and the Father are so completely to be identified with one another that it is impossible to really know one without knowing the other:

John 8:19—"Then they asked him, 'Where is your father?' 'You do not know me or my Father,' Jesus replied. 'If you knew me, you would know my Father also.'"

John 10:30—"I and the Father are one."

John 10:38—"The Father is in me, and I in the Father."

John 12:44, 45—"When a man believes in me, he does not believe in me only, but in the one who sent me. When he looks at me, he sees the one who sent me."

John 10:9, 10—"I am the gate; whoever enters through me will be saved. He will come in and go out, and find pasture. The thief comes only to steal and kill and destroy; I have come that they may have life, and have it to the full."

On the question of our eternal destiny, Jesus leaves us no room for doubt. There is a place in the Father's house, and Jesus is the way to it. Whoever has heard these words and heeds them has nothing to fear in death. He and the Father are one, and as one they have made things ready for us.

I'm not afraid of funerals any longer, but I do dread some of them, especially those in which I'm expected to preach people into Heaven. "He was a good person. He was kind to animals. He once expressed a vague belief in God. Therefore he's in Heaven now." That's what I'm supposed to say. The verses above, however, keep me from making pronouncements like this, for then I would be announcing judgments that only God can make. There is one Son of the living God, One whom the Father sent to rescue the lost, One who is in charge of preparing places for those who follow Him. I can't get around these words, try as I might.

There Is Hope for You (John 14:3)

There is a place, and He prepares it. This is a passage of hope. "I will come back and take you to be with me that you also may be where I am." Is He speaking of His resurrection and return? Probably. Is He speaking of the coming of the Holy Spirit? Again, probably. Is He speaking of His second coming? Probably. All of these probabilities point to what Jesus is really asserting here, which is that our hope is in Him.

When Doris Stone died, leaving her husband Carl after a half a century of marriage, he received many letters of consolation. One of his favorites is this one from his granddaughter:

My Dear Grandpa: I want you to know how much you've been in my thoughts and prayers. I know that this is one of the hardest periods in your life. The only thing I can say is to reach to our Lord and Savior for comfort and encouragement. "For, surely He hath borne our griefs and carried our sorrows . . . He was wounded for our transgressions . . . and with His stripes we are healed." (Isaiah 53:4, 5) Oh, Grandpa, let the Light of Jesus heal your grief and comfort you at this time.

Then she reminisces a bit about her beautiful grandmother and speaks of an anticipated family reunion in the Northwest come summer. Then, after her signature, she adds, "'Surely goodness and mercy shall follow me all the days of my life: and I will dwell in the house of the Lord forever.' Psalm 23:6."

There's a Way for You (John 14:4-6)

How good it is to have Somebody who is the way. Larry and Carol Daily learned this the hard way. They were bound for England, their first time out of the United States, and were a little apprehensive. "Not to worry," I calmed their fears. "I'll be with you the whole time. Stay close to me and I'll take care of you. I am the way!"

Everything went fine until we transferred planes at Kennedy Airport. We waited in the ticket line to be checked in. I went first, since I was to show the way. "Ticket please," the nice lady behind the counter said. I gave her my ticket. "Your passport, please." I gave her my passport. "You can't go to England with this passport," she informed me. I gave her my amazed stare.

The problem was this: I had given her my older, cancelled passport and left my current one at home. Larry and Carol had to fly on to London, where they had never been, without me, to be met by someone they had never seen and who had never seen them. But first they had to fly by themselves, find their luggage in the mass confusion at Heathrow, and go through customs alone. Our church members recall this event clearly, because when they returned, the Dailys pinned on our bulletin board a picture of a disgusted me at Kennedy Airport. Underneath they had penned, "Would you trust this man?" They had, and found me to be untrustworthy.

There are many, many religious hucksters shouting on the television screen and over the airwaves, "Trust me. I am the way. Follow me for the truth and life. I know the way to salvation, I can guarantee you prosperity, I will lead you to an abundant life." They are as incompetent to guide as I was with my expired passport.

Make certain that the one you choose to guide you is worth following.

Jesus' words to His disciples have been about hope and fearlessness in the face of death. We can grant our trust to the One who has gone before us to prepare our place. Through His grace, we can face tomorrow.

This hope is one of God's richest blessings to us. Correspondent Marguerite Higgins learned something of its priceless value as she was covering the fighting in the Korean War. It was forty-two degrees below zero and 18,000 United States Marines were facing 100,000 enemy troops. Among the weary, half-frozen soldiers eating their cold beans from tin cans was a huge Marine, his muddy clothing frozen stiff, his face covered with a long-neglected beard. Ms. Higgins asked him, "If I were God and could grant you anything you wished, what would you like most?"

"Give me tomorrow," he said.[2]

Tomorrow is what Jesus offers. As long as you live on this planet, He invites you to step without fear into tomorrow. Then, when your numbered days on earth are over, He invites you still to step into tomorrow, where there's a place for you.

---

[1]Madeleine l'Engle, *A Circle of Quiet* (New York: Seabury Press, 1972), p. 174.

[2]John Greenlee, "Personally . . . from the Pastor," *Conejo Caller,* (Thousand Oaks, California: First Christian Church), March 26, 1986.